CRYSTAL GAZING

CRYSTAL GAZING

Its History and Practice, with a
Discussion of the Evidence for
Telepathic Scrying

With an Introduction by
ANDREW LANG, M.A., LL.D.

By

NORTHCOTE W. THOMAS, M.A.

Author of " Thought Transference "

ARABI MANOR
REBEL SATORI PRESS
NEW ORLEANS, LOUISIANA
2021

Printed in the United States & United Kingdom by
Arabi Manor, A Rebel Satori Imprint

Originally published in 1905 by
Alexander Morning Limited,
The De La More Press, London

ISBN: 978-1-60864-185-7

CONTENTS

vii

CHAPTER VIII

CHAPTER IX

CHAPTER X

CHAPTER XI

CHAPTER XII

INTRODUCTION

" Do you believe in crystal gazing ? " is a question which one is often asked. One can only reply : " What do you mean by believing in crystal gazing ? If you mean, Do I believe that it is worth while to pay half-a-crown, or a guinea, as a fee to a person who professes to discover by crystal gazing the whereabouts of lost property, or of a missing friend, or to foretell events ?—I do not ' believe in crystal gazing.' " One hears wonderful tales of successes in this kind, but not at first-hand ; and the people who tell them are not very critical, while the practisers are, to begin with, breaking the law. But if the question means, Do I believe that some people have the faculty of seeing faces, places, persons in motion, sometimes recognisable, in a glass ball, or in water, ink, or any clear deep ?—then I do believe in the existence of this faculty. Whether the things thus seen ever answer, except by fortuitous coincidence, to thoughts in another person's mind, things unknown to the crystal gazer, is a different question, to which I return later. But as to the actual existence of an experience which the gazer can only describe as " seeing " such or such things in the glass ball I have no doubt whatever. I shall use for the practice the old English word " scrying "—a form, one may guess, of " descrying." Perhaps I may as well give the grounds of my belief, as far as that belief extends. Like other people, I had heard and read, all my life, of "magic mirrors "—ever since, in childhood, I perused the Notes to " The Lay of the Last Minstrel," and Scott's story, " My Aunt Margaret's Mirror," and Kingsley's Egyptian chapters in " Eothen." Like other people, I thought the stories nothing but mediæval or Oriental romances. But Miss Goodrich-Freer published an essay on crystal gazing in the *Proceedings of the Society for Psychical Research.* The essay contained a brief and interesting history of the practice, and records of personal experiences by the author, " Miss X," whose real name I did not know. I was staying at a hospitable country house, a castle with an ancient legend for being " haunted." None of us ever saw any of the traditional spectres. We sent to London for a glass ball, in which none of us could see anything that was not very natural and normal. The hostess was the last who tried : she found that the ball first yielded mere reflections, then seemed to grow milky, then black, and then pictures appeared. These to some slight degree rather disturbed her equanimity, being novel in her experience, and not corresponding to any conscious thoughts in her mind, which might have suggested them to a person very capable of " visualising "—that is, forming pictures " in her mind's eye " of the object of her conscious thoughts. This power exists in very various degrees, perhaps especially in women, children, and people of genius. Thackeray and Dickens have left descriptions of their own power of visualising : perhaps most imaginative writers possess it, but other writers possess it, who do not seem to be successfully imaginative. The crystal pictures, however, were seen, not " in the mind's eye," but projected outwards into the glass, and did not correspond to any thoughts which the gazer knew that she was thinking, or had ever thought.

This lady's faculty went no further. In perhaps one case she partially beheld the object on which a friend fixed his mind ; in another she saw a curious mystical design that we shortly afterwards found on the cover of a book, recently published, which had not then reached us, and in a third case, when scrying in the crystal cover of a miniature of the Chevalier de St George (James III. and VIII.), she saw what might be explained as the march of his army across the field of Shirramuir. But there was no evidence to anything unusual in such scrys.

I got a glass ball, and, at St Andrews and elsewhere, people of both sexes, and of many social conditions, from my cook of that day (who made the experience casually, as she saw the ball lying about), to golfers, men of business, men of letters, a physician

—all sorts and conditions of men and women, friends, kinsfolk, and chance acquaintances of my own. The proportion of successes in "seeing" crystal pictures was very great—unusually so, I believe. The subject had not then won its way into magazines and general literature and conversation, yet the symptoms, so to say, were identical in cases of success. The ball grew milky, then black; then the pictures appeared, as an almost invariable rule, though the experimenters were not told what to expect, and were quite ignorant of the little that had been written on the topic. I, therefore, took leave to think that all experimenters were not playing on my artless confidence. One lady tried to scry in a glass jug of water. She saw landscapes, an "Ecce Homo," and other things, and doubted whether the Church (she was of the ancient faith) sanctioned the practice. She added, what was curious, that, as a child, she used to spill ink, gaze into it, and see such pictures as she now beheld in the water.

An incident occurred which I have narrated elsewhere. I lent the ball to a Miss Balfour, who only then saw, I think, an old-fashioned piece of furniture. Her brother laughed at her, and took the ball into the study, whence he returned, looking perplexed. He admitted that he had seen a person whom he knew, under a lamp. This was at about 5 P.M., on a Sunday, at St Andrews. He would find out on Tuesday, he said, whether he had seen right or wrong. Miss Balfour told me this. On Tuesday Mr Balfour met, at a dance, in Edinburgh, a lady, Miss Grant.

" On Sunday, at five o'clock," he said, " you were seated under a standard lamp, making tea. A man in blue serge was beside you; his back was towards me; I saw the tip of his moustache. You wore a dress [described] that I never saw you wearing."

" Were the blinds up ? " asked the lady.

" I don't know; I was at St Andrews," said Mr Balfour.

The lady said that all the facts were correct, and she and Mr Balfour wrote out and signed a report of the incident. I had heard Miss Balfour's account of the person seen under a lamp before I learned the conclusion of the story. Not long afterwards Mr Balfour lunched with me. We spoke of " Miss X," Miss Goodrich-Freer and her experiments, on the links before luncheon. Afterwards, in my study, Mr Balfour, who was smoking, gazed into a glass bowl of water. He saw as much of a house as you do see from the hall. The arrangement, as to flooring, doors, windows, and staircase, was of a kind unknown to both of us. A white Persian cat, in the picture, walked down the stairs. The picture lasted long, and I made several changes in the lighting of the room. When I drew down the blind the picture remained, but the large window opposite the front door, in the crystal picture of the house, disappeared.

I happened, later, to meet Miss Goodrich-Freer, whom Mr Balfour had never seen in his life, and told her what he had beheld.

" My house, my Persian cat ! " said the lady.

I had never been in this house, but visited it on my return to town. Mr Balfour's description of what he saw in the picture was absolutely correct, but the Persian cat was out. His existence, however, is amply attested.

Possibly many crystal pictures, unidentified, have their actual model somewhere, but the proto-type, in this case, was discovered by the merest chance. Mr Balfour, a man of strong sense, argued that the picture of the cat was a whiff of tobacco smoke, and the house a thing fancifully constructed out of light, shadows, and reflections. The coinci-dence remained that, out of these, he had " archi-tected " and furnished a house on a system utterly unknown to himself or to me, yet actually existing, and the house was tenanted by a white Persian cat.

The instances which I have given are only a few out of the multitude within my experience. " But your experience," the sceptic will say, " is only that of a listener or a looker-on. You see a man or woman stare at a ring, a jug of water, a glass bowl, the ink in an inkpot, or what not ; the person who stares then tells you that he or she sees this or that picture, whereas he sees no picture at all in the crystal. Either he is merely practising on your credulity, or he honestly believes that he sees what he says he sees, but does not see. In the latter case, to put the matter as it is usually stated : ' It is all imagination.' "

At this point may I take it as conceded that all my friends, kinsfolk, and acquaintances who tell me that they see pictures in the glass ball are not mere practical jokers, playing on my credulity ? Really, they are so numerous, and many of them are such grave substantial characters, and their experiences, as described, agree with each other in so many points, that I think it would only be fair to exclude the hypothesis of hoaxing, as a general rule.

This point I am anxious to secure, and in proof I wish to cite the behaviour of some of the people whom I have observed. Some six years ago I was staying in early spring at a Highland hotel, when very few visitors had assembled. With me was a young kinswoman, or " kinsgirl," Miss Gregor, whom I had known since her childhood ; she was healthy, veracious, and, as far as becomes her sex, athletic. She had just found out that she could see pictures in a glass ball. At the dinner-table with us were two young Englishmen, strangers to us. They tried the glass ball, and, finding that they had the faculty of " scrying," or seeing pictures, were interested, and made some experiments in their own rooms. One tried looking at the ball in darkness, at night. He said that it seemed to become of a fiery quality, glowing bright, but in these conditions he saw no pictures in the glow. By daylight or artificial light he saw pictures, usually of people known to him, and members of his family. One lady, he said, he saw always in an inverted position, as when you look at the sitter through a photographic camera. I have not found another example of this eccentricity. The remarks appeared to be candid, and the experiment in the dark was like that of another friend, an engineer, who tried excluding all light, and gazing into a funnel. The field of vision, in his case, became luminous, and pictures appeared.

Evidence of this kind must be " subjective "; we have only the word of the experimenter for it. But we have only people's words for all subjective psychological facts, such as " coloured audition " (the association of colours with sounds), the viewing of numerals in colours and symmetric patterns, the arabesques seen by Herschel, and so forth.

Miss Gregor, in one of her earliest experiments, saw very distinctly Dunstaffnage Castle, the old home of the Dalriada kings, near Oban, which we had been visiting. She also saw a lady, well known to both of us, sitting alone, and playing at a card game, in which little bags of counters are used.

She had once seen the lady playing at this game in company, but we found, on inquiry, that the lady had, in fact, been playing alone, for the first time, just before the picture was seen in the glass ball. No doubt this was a merely accidental coincidence.

We then tried the usual experiment, myself and Miss Hamilton being present. Miss Hamilton was to think ; Miss Gregor was to see the object of her thought. Miss Gregor saw a lady, " like your mother, but not your mother. Her complexion is ruddy, her eyes are brown, she is dressed in black, her hair is white," and she described the *coiffure*. I at once recognised the description, that of a lady well known to me, whom Miss Gregor had never seen. " It is right," said Miss Hamilton ; " I was thinking of my aunt, my mother's sister."

We then called in a Mr Brown to do the thinking. Miss Gregor then saw the two young Englishmen already mentioned (who had left), fishing in a boat on the loch.

" I began by fixing my mind on them," said Mr Brown, " but at the last I was thinking of the big trout they caught."

This was a kind of success. So we tried next day, Mrs Hamilton as thinker. Miss Gregor saw her daughter Marjory, then in London, painting at an easel, in a blue linen smock. But Mrs Hamilton had been thinking of a favourite dog, and Marjory did not even possess a blue smock to cover

b

her dress when painting. Then I tried. What I thought of I forget, but what Miss Gregor saw was— John Knox. Later, I remembered that, some days before, I had thought of John Knox, but Miss Gregor had seen something else. She did not remember this, and I forgot it too, till after an interval of some hours. We all taunted Miss Gregor as " a fraudulent medium," which she " took very unconcernedly," as the Christian carrier " took his shooting by Claverhouse's dragoons." Out of four attempts she had missed twice, once scored a bull's eye, and once an outer.

As in many other cases, her efforts were wont to be " there or thereabouts." In her experiment with her mother she saw a back view of that lady and a friend, Mrs Black, standing in a great hall, looking upward : at what they were looking she did not know. But what Mrs Gregor was thinking of was the tall " Haida totem post," in the hall of the Anthropological Museum at Oxford, which, some weeks earlier, she had visited in company with the lady here styled Mrs Black. It is a gigantic post, carved with the totemic armorial quarterings of a Haida gentleman, and originally erected in front of his hut, as is the custom. Thus Miss Gregor was in close but not absolutely perfect contact with her mother's reflections, much as in the case of the men in the boat and the big trout. Whether these coincidences were mere chance work, or had some other origin, everyone may decide according to his taste and fancy. But, out of the whole universe of things thinkable, Miss Gregor made good shots in three out of five cases given ; she had a " memory picture " of a thing forgotten by both of us in the John Knox case ; and, in Mrs Hamilton's case, the picture seems to have been the result of a guess, conscious or subconscious.

Another spontaneous and successful " seeing " of Miss Gregor's was the most remarkable known to me, as it involved the successful discernment of a string of names and numerals, and was thoroughly well attested. But in this instance no glass ball was used, the names and numerals appeared as if written on a black-board, no effort having been made to see them in the mind's eye.

These experiments were, of course, unscientific, and undertaken for mere idle amusement. The method of statistics was not applied ; there were not, in my knowledge, more experiments made than those which I have chronicled, with one other, on the same level of success as the affair of the totem post. One case, we have seen, was not an experiment.

To amuse an eminent *savant* and me, Miss Gregor looked into a ball, while nobody directed his mind to anything in particular. Miss Gregor saw a very tall savage, with a still taller bow, such as she had never beheld, nor I either, for that matter. Next day our friend pointed out to us in a museum a Patagonian bow which "answered to pattern." The fact that he is an anthropologist would naturally attract Miss Gregor's mind to savages, whose bows, except in the Patagonian case, are usually short, though she probably did not know it.

Everyone can see that, to prove, in Miss Gregor's case, that her mind is, in some unknown way, in contact with the minds of the experimenters who do the thinking, hundreds, perhaps thousands, of careful experiments must be made, and the proportion of bull's eyes, centres, outers, and misses must be recorded. Not being a mathematician, I do not know how many failures and outers, out of five hundred experiments, would prove the centres and bull's eyes to be the mere result of chance coincidence. But the field of possible errors is coexistent with the thinkable universe—that is, the person who does the thinking may choose any one of millions of things unknown to the crystal gazer. If, then, the crystal gazer is right in a considerable percentage of cases, to my unmathematical mind it does look as if some unknown human faculty and fact in nature may be surmised. If this be so, it may be presumed that some quality in the mind of the thinker as well as of the gazer must be in tune if the experiment is to be successful.

I may be an idle enthusiast, but I cannot help thinking that some official professor of psychology might make experiments. He would, if successful, be treated as M. Blondlot, of the " N-rays," is used by many of his learned colleagues ; but, if his experiments were dead failures, he would have his reward, and his name would be great in the scientific Israel. At present the position of M. Blondlot, whether he is in the right, or whether he is *un pauvre halluciné* (as Dr Janet said of a lady often mentioned in this book), cannot be called enviable. But Lady Mary Wortley Montague, and Jenner, and Braid, and Elliston, and Simpson, had troubles from learned colleagues to face in the matters of inoculation, vaccination, hypnotism, and chloroform.

One very eminent professor of psychology told me, some years ago, that he could not find anyone who professed to see even fancy pictures in a glass ball. My experience is different, but I am so lazy ! I have just passed a month under the roof of a relation who, in a solitary experiment made some time ago, " saw " ; but I had not a glass ball, and did not know how to procure one, not being aware that they are kept in stock, as Mr Thomas tells us, by the Society for Psychical Research, 20 Hanover Square. The glass jug of water has inconveniences in practice, and many people who can " see " in glass balls cannot " see " in ink.

So far, I have mainly been arguing that all my " scryers " are not practical jokers. In corroboration, when I examined savage practice, and bar-

baric and ancient practice, I found that from the Australian black fellows to the Maoris, the Samoyeds, the Iroquois, the Incas, the Aztecs, the Malagasies, the negroes, the Arabs, the Egyptians, the Greeks, and the mediæval European nations, all were crystal gazers. If they saw no pictures at all in crystals, polished basalt, obsidian mirrors, blood drops, ink, water, livers of animals, and so on, it is not in nature that all should go on " scrying." They must have made the discovery of the faculty by accident, like the lady already mentioned, who, as a child, amused herself by " scrying " in ink ; and like George Sand, who, in childhood, used the polished back of a screen, and appears never to have heard of any other instance of the practice.

I do not think we can state the facts at a lower level than this :

Some persons can, and others cannot, " see " pictures, not voluntarily or consciously evoked and " visualised," in a smooth deep. This is a circumstance in human psychology quite as curious as the visions of coloured lines of numerals, established by Mr Francis Galton. But official psychologists, as a rule, avoid the subject. Are they influenced by an aversion to the inquiry as to whether the things seen, in some cases, appear to reflect the unknown thought of a party to the experiment ? That way, to be sure, lies " the occult," a word rendered terrific by silly enthusiasts. In merely examining crystal gazing we are on the border of the realm of quackery, fraud, blind credulity, avid hopes, and superstitious fears. There is no doubt at all that, this border once crossed, even minds practised in the physical sciences often cease to be scientific or sensible. I have read, with distaste, the credulities and wild speculations published (about affairs beyond the border) by more than one man of eminence in this or that field of orthodox science. The lucubrations of other *savants* who have just peeped across the border in a spirit of cursing, like that of Balaam, are often more entertaining, so reckless are these gentlemen, sometimes, of accuracy and even of honesty—the dishonesty being "subconscious," no doubt. Thus we can explain the aversion of men of science to the examination of phenomena—no more offensive, really, than the dreams of the day or the night. They are phenomena of human nature, exercises of human faculty, and, as such, invite study. To shirk examination is less than courageous.

If I have proved, or made it highly probable, that all my crystal gazers are not practical jokers, there remains the theory that "it is all imagination." But what is "imagination"? How do you define it, and how does your definition apply to the case?

Most people, if they get beyond the theory that all folk who say they can see pictures in glass balls and so forth are liars, remark: " It is just imagination." To ask such sceptics: " What is imagination? How do you define it?" is cruel, for they have always been contented with the word, and have never reflected on its sense. I turn away from the notion of asking any person to *think*! The exercise is repugnant to the natural man.

We may, perhaps, find out what the public mean by " imagination" if we examine the senses in which the word is currently used. We explain, in common talk, the tales which a child, or which many grown-ups, tell about their own adventures by saying that they are " imaginative." The child tells you of his adventures with sharks in the pond or bears in the garden. He has heard or read of bears and sharks, and he has made a romance about them, in which himself is the hero. Vanity and the nascent literary impulse inspire him. A man tells you of his successes among the fair, or among trout or deer. In the former case he is a cur or a liar or a fatuous fool; in the second case you cannot tell whether he is " romancing " or speaking truth without considerable knowledge of his character and qualities. He may be veracious, and yet a listener who does not know by personal experience the strange chances of hill and wood and stream, says to himself: " The man is imaginative"; just as he would say of the man who sees crystal pictures. Very probably the sportsman is telling the actual truth, and a fellow-sportsman believes him. He is reckoned " imaginative " only by listeners who have not lived alone with nature and wild things. In the same way, the listener who has never inquired into crystal gazing thinks the scryer " imaginative," yet he may no more be " imaginative " than the sportsman is. He may be only narrating matters not in the experience of the listener. To this extent, then, we may discount the popular theory of " it is all imagination."

Again, we use the word " imagination," commonly, of the constructive faculty of the poet or artist. He broods on a theme, let us say, till he " sees " it with " that inner eye which is the bliss of solitude," with his " mind's eye," and then he reproduces, in words, sounds, clay, or colours, what he has " seen," reproduces it with more or less success.

This we call " constructive imagination," and it is exerted with purpose, and with full consciousness, as a rule. We all exercise, or try to exercise, this faculty when " on the dark we strive to paint " the face of a friend or the aspect of a landscape. The power exists in various degrees. I, for one, am almost without it. We call the process " visualising." Now, some crystal gazers (*see* p. 41 below) can visualise a face, say, " in the mind's eye," and then transfer the picture into the crystal. I do not know if this power is common. However, let us suppose it to be common. Next let us suppose that, in an experiment, A does the thinking, B guesses at the object of A's thought, " visualises " what he has guessed at, and transfers the mental picture to the crystal. The guess may be right (as in the case of Miss Hamilton's aunt) or wrong (as in the case of Miss Hamilton's sister, *see* p. xviii. above). In the instance of the aunt, Miss Gregor had never seen her, but she *may* have seen her photograph, guessed that Miss Hamilton was thinking of her, and then made a mental picture of the photograph, invented the colouring, and transferred it to the crystal.

In this case we have a lucky guess at Miss Hamilton's thought—a very lucky guess—for the lady had the whole universe to expatiate in, " in maiden meditation, fancy free." Secondly, we have an effort of a recognised form of imagination—namely, " visualisation." Thirdly, Miss Gregor puts the mental picture into the crystal, or says that she does—persuades herself that she does so : here all is conscious, purposeful work of the imagination.

Again, in the case of the totem post, Miss Gregor knew that her mother had seen the post, in company with Mrs Black. She *guessed*, let us say, that of this visit to the museum her mother was thinking, and she guessed right. But why did she guess that the two ladies were looking upward in the large hall, and not guess that they were looking at the

totem post, a point which would have made her conjecture much more telling ?   I do not know ; but,
in any case, granting these explanations, we see
how the thing works—namely, first by a conscious
and lucky guess, next by conscious exercise of the
faculty of imagination—or of untruthful assertion !
If I guess that you are thinking of Mr Chamberlain
I can pretend that I see Mr Chamberlain in the
crystal though I see no picture at all.   Thus we
eliminate even " imagination," and fall back on
robust falsehood and lucky conjecture.   Only
those who, from long acquaintance with the scryer,
believe him incapable of " larking," need any other
explanation.   " Imagination "   is   superfluous !
The successes are accidents.   This argument brings
us back to the sceptical starting-point—" Scryers
are liars."   But I really cannot repeat my reasons
for not accepting this rather crude explanation.

There is another sense, in which the theory that
crystal gazers are not mendacious, but are victims
of " mere imagination," has some sense in it.   Most
people, I presume, when looking drowsily at the fire
in the grate, at the clouds in the sky, at the dis-
coloured patches on a wall, or at the pattern of a
wall paper not distinctly beheld, see resemblances
to castles, towns, hills, faces, whales—like Hamlet—
and any other things.   Here " imagination " is
busy.   Now, it may be contended that crystal
gazers construct, or compose what they see in the

glass, partly consciously and partly unconsciously out of points and planes of light and shadow in the crystal, and out of the distorted reflections of objects in the room. To do this requires more " imagination " than those of us possess who cannot see crystal pictures, but can construct a kind of fancy resemblance to faces, animals, and mountains out of the light in the embers, the clouds in the sky, and the splashes and stains on a plastered wall. I am very willing to admit that " imagination " in this sense—namely, the imaginative construction of a picture out of the lights, shadows, and reflections in the glass—may be the actual cause of some crystal-picture seeings. Almost anybody can turn the ball about till he gets a view of a frozen lake bordered by snowy hills. Of course, the person who does this knows what he is doing, knows that he is making up his landscape intentionally. But if a band of skaters suddenly begins to circle about on the glassy lake of the landscape thus composed that is a very different thing; yet such crystal pictures of moving figures are constantly reported by crystal gazers. These cannot be explained in the theory that imagination is active, merely as it is when we see, in a blotch on a wall, a likeness, say, to a man preaching. For the figure on the wall is motionless ; the skaters are in motion.

The real process in crystal gazing is much more like that of watching visions of faces, places, and other things, with closed eyes, between sleeping and waking. These visions are technically called "hypnagogic illusions," which means illusive appearances introducing sleep. (*See* Mr Thomas, pp. 17, 18.)

As Mr Thomas touches very briefly on these things I shall be more ample. Hypnagogic illusions appear to be matters of less common experience than a person familiar with them, like myself, might suppose. Probably most people, happy people, fall sound asleep almost as soon as their head touches the pillow. They have no *illusions hypnagogiques*. These are, in my own case, sudden uprisings of unknown faces before the closed eyes. The faces are often beautiful at first, but fleet through a series of changes to the grotesque and the hideous, so that I have to open my eyes to get rid of them. They change and pass with extreme celerity. As a rule, I repeat, the faces are almost always unknown, but I once saw myself in profile. I cannot, when awake, summon up mental pictures of known faces, or but very dimly, while these little illusions of drowsy, shut eyes are often very brilliant. Sometimes when they occur I try to call up "the face I shall not see," or rather the faces, now so many, of those whom we have lost awhile. But this proves impossible. The unknown, the uncalled for, the unexpected strange faces, fair or hideous, sweep past; never, never once, the faces of our desire, though these may visit us in actual dreams of sleep. The same remark holds good of landscapes and inanimate things : those which I see have always been unknown to me, or, if once known, are lost to memory, except in a single in - stance. I had visited Carlisle Castle, and remarked the heraldic bearings carved in miniature on the door lintels by prisoners of old. Not long after- wards I saw them distinctly in a hypnagogic illusion, just as Miss Gregor saw Dunstaffnage Castle and the card-playing lady in an early experiment with the glass ball.

Now, in my own case, I can occasionally observe the geneses of these hypnagogic phantasms. On closing the eyes we, or most of us, see floating, shifting, vanishing specks or little blotches of light of various colours, formless and fleeting. I can, when half asleep, watch one of these specks or blotches growing, in an infinitesimal space of time, into a face, or other recognisable form of any sort, changing to another, quite unlike the first ; to a third, and so on. I cannot command or modify the forms, that is done by some faculty of half slumber which is not directed by any will or desire. Again, shapes of printed letters, black on white, arise, and are legible ; and I have seen a very remarkable wall pattern in crimson, which I could not, when wide awake, invent or design. This morning my hypna- gogic illusions took the shape of an inscription in characters, of which some seemed Hebrew, others early Greek. I had not been working at the origin of the alphabet for more than a year, but yesterday I had mentioned the subject of early writing to a friend. All this kind of phantasmagoria beheld between sleeping and waking is very closely analogous to the picture beheld by crystal gazers. Some of them, not many (Mr Thomas names Mrs Verrall), can trace the genesis of the crystal picture to actual points of light and dark in the glass, just as I can sometimes see the speck of colour before the shut eyes develop into the changeful face.

If Mrs Verrall's experience were that of crystal gazers in general (as, perhaps, it really is, though they have not consciously observed it), then we might have a theory. We might say that crystal pictures are, unconsciously and unintentionally, constructed by them out of points of light and dark in the glass, the gazers being wide awake, just as *illusions hypna-gogiques* are, unintentionally and unconsciously, constructed out of blurs and specks of colour in the shut eyes, by myself and others, when half asleep. (*See* Alfred Maury, " Le Sommeil et les Rêves.")

Some length this theory carries us ; but there is a great deal of difference between being half asleep and being wide awake ! I must insist that, out of scores of cases of crystal gazers who saw crystal pictures, I have never met one who was other than wide awake during the process, talking and describing, criticising, leaving off scrying to take tea, or smoking without leaving off. Very possibly to stare at a fixed object may make some people drowsy, but it has not been so in any case within my personal experience. I have stared vainly at a glass ball for long, and many a time, but no more felt sleepy than I saw pictures.

I was once able to test the theory of reflections converted into pictures in a curious way. The Mr Balfour already spoken of (page xiii) was very sceptical about his own powers. " As to the vision of Miss Grant at a tea-table," he argued, " I knew it was tea-time, and translated some reflection in the glass into Miss Grant making tea."

" And the man in blue serge, and the dress you did not know that she possessed ? "

These appearances Mr Balfour did not explain. At the time of this conversation two young ladies who could " scry " were on a visit in the neighbourhood. They were acquaintances of mine, not of Mr Balfour's, who himself was on a visit to the place. These ladies had been witnesses, or percipients, with their mother and others, collectively and simultaneously, of a truly appalling spectre, seen one evening in a place where early next morning, a terrible disaster occurred, with loss of several lives. They told me the tale, and the phantasm was of such a novel type, so unconventional, that I made sceptical observations.

Even Professor Ray Lankester, if I know him, would have gone so far as to " hint a doubt and hesitate dislike " of the reported appearance. My tone irritated the ladies, and as *I* believed in " scrying," *they* declared that " scrys " were " only reflections in the glass." I then arranged an experiment. I would bring two glass balls, and introduce Mr Balfour. I brought in Mr Balfour, and one of the ladies " scryed " with her back to the window. Mr Balfour was stationed at the other end of the room, beside the door. Both scryers indicated that they had " seen." I took Mr Balfour out of the room, along a passage, beyond earshot. He had seen an old woman, seated at a table. We returned to the drawing-room, and asked the lady what *she* had seen. She also had seen an old woman, standing up. There was no old woman in the room to be reflected, and the reflections of the two opposite ends of the rooms were not likely to coincide in being construable into an old woman—in one scry seated, in the other standing up—probably not the same old woman. Collusion was barred, as the two parties to the experiments were entire strangers to each other.

We have advanced, or I have advanced, whatever the reader may have done, to this point, that crystal pictures are analogous to *waking* hypnagogic illusions—a contradiction in terms ! It is no great strain on credulity to believe that a scryer, by concentrating attention on a given point of vision, when awake, may have experiences analogous to, but usually much more durable than, the visual experiences of other persons on the margin of sleep. This theory would be much more easy of acceptance if I could say that my scrying acquaintances are drowsy when engaged in scrying, but they have invariably been, to all appearance, absolutely and normally wide awake.

We now come to a topic already touched upon in the cases of Mr Balfour and Miss Gregor—the perception by scryers of real persons, or places, unknown to them, and distant, though, perhaps, present to the mind of the person who does the thinking in the experiment. If this kind of crystal picture could be statistically tested, and if successes occurred in a sufficient proportion of experiments (whatever that proportion ought to be), we should be in sight, I presume, of a result. Some cause, of a nature hitherto unascertained, would, apparently, determine the visions of the scryer which coincide with the thought of the person who does the thinking. Whether we christen the cause, or process, by the name of " telepathy " or " thought transference " or " K-rays," is a matter purely indifferent. We should be no nearer to understanding the process, or processes. " What nearer is it " if we mix up M. Blondlot's " N-rays " (actual or imaginary) with the coincidence of A's thought and B's scry ?

We might as logically say "Humpty-Dumpty is Abracadabra." We would be " paying ourselves with words." An " N-ray " is not a phase of human consciousness ; a thought *is* a phase of human consciousness, " that you may lay to," says Captain Cuttle. What our inquiry demands is proof of actual and constant, not casual and sporadic, co-incidence between A's unrevealed thought and B's scry. We require a long series of experiments, not with a scryer who has seen nothing more than unidentifiable crystal pictures, but with scryers known to be at least on the level of Miss Gregor. The proper persons to make such experiments are accredited professors of psychology, and nobody else. What a casual amateur like myself may observe and record is of no scientific value, unless it has the effect of encouraging experiment by specialists.

My own " classical " instance is the case of Miss Angus, to whom Mr Thomas refers (pp. 141-144). He has not selected her cases which most impressed myself. They are published in my " Making of Religion," and I still possess the MS. records, attestations, and signatures. I myself introduced the subject of crystal gazing to Miss Angus, who had never heard of it before, and during the three or four weeks in which we were in the habit of meeting, her successes were numerous and peculiar, while of failures at that time I only heard of a few:

once when she saw nothing; once or twice with myself, and once with a lady who is herself a " scryer," and a seeress. One failure was when I asked her to describe the study of a correspondent in Algiers, which I had never seen. The description seemed so improbable that I never asked my French friend whether it were wrong or right. Miss Angus was not told his name, place of residence, profession, or nationality. This experiment, in popular phrase, was " trying Miss Angus rather high," for I have never seen my foreign correspondent (an eminent Egyptologist), nor did I try to fix my mind on a person whom I had never seen. On reviewing the past, I seem also to remember that Mr F. W. H. Myers told me that Miss Angus was unsuccessful in his case.

Perhaps I had better mention all our own triasl. On the first occasion, the second time of our meeting, at a tea-party, I asked Miss Angus " to see what I wanted her to see," adding that I would fix my mind elsewhere—namely, on a card in a pack—and that a Mr Johnstone, an undergraduate, would guess at the card. He guessed the ace of hearts, which was the card I had selected. Meanwhile Miss Angus, seated at some distance off, was looking at the glass ball. She described the remote object which I wanted her to see very minutely, adding an important detail which was not in my knowledge. I thought that this must be an error, but on making inquiries in the proper quarter I found that it was correct. I confess that on this occasion (and on only one other in my life) a feeling of chill seemed to run down my spine !

On the other hand, some weeks later, when I fixed my mind on an attempt to visualise Mr W. G. Grace in cricket costume, Miss Angus saw a limping old man. Thirdly, I had acquired some " lammer beads " (amber beads), once the property of one of the Paisley witches, burned for bewitching Miss Christian Shaw of Bargarran, the founder of the Renfrewshire thread industry. I wrote to Miss Angus, who was at a distance, asking her to scry " to the intention of some amber beads." What she saw was a lady and two men, " in old-fashioned costume," in a room which had the air of being a chamber in a prison. Certainly I do not say that this was Miss Shaw, with two friends, waiting in the prison where Margaret Lang and six other victims accused of sorcery were examined and tortured. In this case too Miss Angus was " tried rather high."

One other experiment, one which closes our account, was at least picturesque. We visited the ruined archiepiscopal castle of St Andrews. Miss Angus sat down, with the glass ball, in the large, roofless chamber on the first floor, while I walked about in the grassy court. I expected the lady, if she saw anything, to see a fancy picture of the murder of Cardinal Beaton in May 1546. But the pictures were these : a man in one of the tall, conical black hats, such as the Regent Morton wears in his portrait, walking up an avenue. Next, that picture passing, came " a lady in a crinoline, without a ruff."

" In a crinoline ! " I said, disappointed.

" Yes ; she is pale, stands with her hand on the back of a chair, the skirt of her dress is of such or such a colour [grey silk brocade], and the crinoline is of such and such a shape." I forget the precise words.

" That's not a crinoline, it is a farthingale," I said ; but about farthingales Miss Angus was uninstructed. This mode of distending the dress was very fashionable in Scotland in the sixteenth century. Knox, writing to two godly sisters who consulted him on the ethics of costume, gave them a pleasing latitude as to gold and velvet, " but I think that farthingalis cannot be justifeit."

When Miss Angus had described the costume I said : " I think you have spotted Mariotte Ogilvy."

She had never heard of Mariotte, a lady of the House of Airlie, who lived with the Cardinal as his wife, the *liaison* being accepted by society, and the children marrying into the noblest families. Now, Knox tells us that Mariotte was in the castle with the Cardinal on the night before his murder ; and as I was working at the history of the period my mind

had dwelt on the emotions of the poor lady when
the news reached her, in the early morning, that
        " Stickit was the Cardinal,
        And sauted like ane sow "—
as the Protestant rhyme ran. But as to how the
lady would be dressed I had never thought of asking.
We went straight to the University Library, and
consulted a book on costume as to the attire of
ladies about 1546. The coloured print of female
array for that period corroborated the crystal
picture : it was very correct.

The coincidence was, at all events, pretty ; and
the " scry " was of an unexpected nature, for one
would have expected the scryer either to " see "
the murder scene, or some other less universally
known incident of the castle's history, or something
wholly unconnected with it, or nothing at all, as
occasionally occurs. But there *was* a connection,
shadowy if you please ; nay, if you please, a connection existing only for myself ; and I accept Miss
Angus's ignorance of the existence of Mariotte, who
is not mentioned in the guide's description of the
castle's history. She is a lady remembered by few
except her actual collateral descendants, one of
whom is named after her.

A selection of Miss Angus's numerous successes,
as Mr Thomas says, is given in a book of mine
already mentioned. One case, unpublished, was
of a " sensational " nature, in connection with a

lost object of value. But the incidents, for reasons which seem insuperable, cannot be offered. I have tried to give an analogous account, changing the details, but the result would be unsatisfactory

As a reference to my book will prove, Miss Angus's " scrys " showed the strange vagaries of the faculty. One example is given by Mr Thomas (pp. 142, 143). Miss Angus " saw " not the man thought of by the lady who did the thinking, but his mother. Now, when a lady does the thinking, if we merely guess, we guess at a man as the object of her contemplations, like, in the converse case, the Arab boy who saw a lovely, golden-haired, azure-eyed girl, when Kinglake was thinking of the flogging Eton headmaster, Dr Keate. In two cases noted, Miss Angus " saw " what was in the mind of a person in the room who was taking no part in the experiment ; in one of these instances she also hit on the object of the thoughts of the experimenter.

But much the most extraordinary feature in her experiments was her success, not only in describing the person thought of, but the actual dress and circumstances of that person (unknown to her even by name) at the moment of the scry. Once, even more strangely, she described, and in one case mimicked, the gait of one of the persons in the mind of the thinker, with their occupations and environment (Oriental). This was on a Saturday night in Scotland. The post on Sunday brought a letter of one of the persons seen, from India, and the letter (which I read) described the occupations and environment discerned by Miss Angus, which, at the moment of the scry, were several weeks remote in time. Had Miss Angus known the person described (of whom she had never heard), and read the undelivered letter, she could not have been more accurate. Another instance of the same kind is given. Miss Angus saw a person, unknown to her, but much in the mind of another person present, a complete stranger to Miss Angus, not engaged in the experiment, in an attitude very unusual, but actually assumed by the distant person described some hours earlier in the day than the moment of the crystal gazing.

In the great majority of cases known to me the experiments were made with entire strangers, or with the most recent of acquaintances. In no case was there physical contact with the thinker; scryer and thinker did not touch each other; there could, therefore, be no " muscle-reading." Indeed, once, when, by the thinker's desire, they clasped hands, only scurrying blurs were seen in the glass ball. The general impression left by this lady's experiments was that, for her, time and space " broke adrift." I ought to add that, in no case within my knowledge, was any effort made to " scry " the future; while I was the only person concerned who suggested the attempt at a glimpse into the past, in the instance of the amber beads, and the castle —in that case the scene was left to do what it could with its own suggestions. In the Indian case, the scry appeared to be " retrospective "—the events described were of the recent past.

I can form no shadow of a theory as to the causes and processes conceivably at work in this group of experiments.

If anyone says that Miss Angus's mind is somehow in touch with the mind of the other experimenter, how does that account for her apparent vision of actual facts unknown to that person ? I have given all such instances of failure as I witnessed or heard of, and, of course, many of the people concerned would have been glad to report failures, as I would have been keen to mark them : I do not record all the successes. In one instance, not recorded in writing at the time, the conflict of memories is of the most curious kind. If I may trust my own memory, which in these matters is good, one learned man was a partner to two experiments at some interval of time. One was a success, in the other case nothing was seen in the ball. All the details of the success (the person descried was in Canada) are vividly present to my mind. But my friend only remembers the instance in which nothing was seen, which Miss Angus, being consulted, also remembered. The other case came back to her memory when I jogged it ; but such a recollection is not evidence. Did I invent the successful experiment, the name of the lady descried (a person of rank, whom I have only once seen, but who is a friend of the partner to the experiment), the large, empty, lighted-up room of state in which she stood, the snow in the streets, the sleighs in the snow ? Three or four years ago I spoke of the experiment to the learned person who did the thinking, and who, in my memory, told the story to me, at the time, hard by the castle of St Andrews. He denied that it had ever occurred. Last year I again mentioned it. He again denied that it had occurred, and also denied that I had mentioned it to him two or three years before. Am I " a dommed leear," like the Peebles man of the story ; or is my friend's memory, at this point, defective ? Perhaps I am much more inventive than I give myself credit for ; but as I take a plentiful lack of interest in Lady K (the person descried—in my memory), I did not even know that she *was* in Canada till I heard the story, which my friend (in *his* memory) never told.

There was such plenty of stories at the time that I did not take the trouble to make a written record, as was usually done. It should *always* be done, both in the case of successes and failures. But there is little use, or none, in making experiments as to the possibility of discovery of hidden thoughts, with a crystal gazer who habitually sees nothing but fancy pictures or memory pictures. I need hardly say that, if a scryer often " sees " correctly, and often things wholly unknown to him before the scry, this is in itself a proof that he *does* " see," and is not merely inventing or " imagining." I may be asked : What sort of people are most apt to see crystal pictures ? I never tried experiments with children, very young people, or unhealthy, fanciful, and " hysterical " people. It seems probable that persons with strong powers of " visualising," or seeing things in the " mind's eye," are most likely to succeed, but they often fail entirely. Again, whoever has had, though sane and healthy, one or more waking hallucinations, such as seeing, within doors, and in a good light, a person who is absent, or non-existent, seems, *prima facie*, apt to make a scryer. On these terms I ought to be able to scry, but I cannot. Miss A was apt to see waking hallucinations that corresponded to facts not known to her, and other hallucinations in " haunted houses " : she scrys very well. Mr B, a painter, and a strong visualiser, who has had ghostly experiences in a " haunted house " (his own), could not scry : he found that the glass ball became milky or misty, but no pictures appeared.

Miss C, a lady of great humour and strength of character, who has seen waking hallucinations, and merely laughs at them, can see crystal pictures occasionally, but not often, and I understand that they are always unidentifiable fancy pictures or revived memories. In one case she saw a friend in the act of writing a letter, and a letter reached her from the friend a post or two later; but that was not a notable coincidence. Thus I really cannot guess as to what sort of person is or is not likely, *prima facie*, to see crystal pictures. I may think Professor Ray Lankester an unlikely person; he may think me a likely person, but I cannot scry, and possibly he can : it is a point on which I have no information. Miss Gregor seemed to me, *prima facie*, one of the most unlikely people in the world to be able to scry, and as much may be said of Miss Angus. One has a notion that the born scryer is a pallid, anæmic girl, with large, mysterious eyes, hollow cheeks, untidy hair, and a strong aversion to exercise in the open air. But the scryers whom I know are healthy, jolly people, young, middle-aged, or more than middle-aged. They usually take little interest in the whole affair; and as to philosophy about telepathy, N-rays, the ether, the subliminal self, and so forth, they pay no attention to the theorists and their propounders. They are not spiritualists, are not theosophists, and never bore one with " the astral plane," " cerebral centres," and other such jargon. I only once saw a professional medium play with a crystal ball ; he appeared to be a harmless being, possibly half-witted, and he " saw " little or nothing, but what he described as " confusions."

I handed to him a Jeanne d'Arc ring, with the inscription: Maria, I. H. S., and he said he saw a middle-aged lady in black, who certainly had no obvious connection with anything in particular. For others who were with me he saw " confusions." We pitied, and forsook him—" a foolish old man, who did not even understand his own foolish old business."

" And what do you really think of *your* foolish old business ? " asks the candid reader, or, if a lady, inquires : " Do you believe in crystal gazing ? " The question is unphilosophical in form, but I reply to what it is intended to mean. I believe that some crystal gazers are, somehow, enabled to " see " things which are actual, but of which, crystal gazing apart, they have, and can have, no knowledge. I have no conjecture as to " how it is done " ; but, if it *is* done, it upsets some extant popular philosophies. People are apt to think that a thing is explained when they are familiar with something analogous to it. The processes described are analogous to " wireless telegraphy," on the Marconi system. But the analogy explains nothing. If a number of people are in a room, the brains of all are busy endlessly. If the activity of the brain sets up " currents," electrical or other, how does the current of the person scryed for come to be selected by the receiver in the brain of the scryer? There are exceptions, as in two of Miss Angus's cases—her cerebral receiver picked up brain currents from persons to whose intention she was not scrying. The phenomena are quite as curious and important as those of radium, but, as they cannot be produced at will on every occasion, as they are capricious in appearance, being subject to laws not ascertained, I do not expect them to be scientifically examined for many a long year, if ever.

But my last word is, take not your opinion from mine. An ex-president of the Folklore Society has informed me that the phenomena entirely depend on a disordered liver, to which I can only reply that, if it be so, I should be the chief of scryers. The questions at issue can only be settled after many long series of experiments conducted by psychological specialists, working with sane and healthy subjects—British subjects for choice.

CRYSTAL GAZING

CHAPTER I

SUPERSTITION AND INCREDULITY

" I AM glad to say my people are not superstitious,"
said a worthy Welsh clergyman to a friend of mine,
a good folklorist, now, alas, no more, and went on
to explain that there were no ghosts in the parish.
His joy was damped, it is true, half-an-hour later,
when his guest inquired of the school children which
of them could tell him where a *bwggan* was to be
seen, and found there was not a child in the school
but could put him on the track of one.

It is very commonly said that it is superstitious
to believe in ghosts and crystal gazing and "such
rubbish." Many otherwise worthy people absolutely refuse to credit the fact that some of their
fellow-creatures, quite as veracious as themselves,
may be able to see and hear what they cannot, or,
rather, may have what are technically termed
hallucinations, and may consequently be neither
liars nor superstitious when they say they have seen
a ghost, or successfully "scryed" in a crystal ball
or a glass of water.

A

When we ask incredulous persons to explain wherein the superstition consists it is by no means easy to get an explicit reply. While ghost seeing *may* be a result of suggestion, and depend on the belief that the souls of the deceased forefathers of the hamlet are wandering round the village church-yard at midnight to scare the bold wight who ventures forth, it by no means follows that all ghost seers hold that view, or that they " believe " in ghosts at all, whatever that may mean.

Since the International Census of 1889-92 no one in his senses can doubt that a considerable number of sane and healthy people, otherwise indistinguish-able from their fellows, occasionally see visions or hear sounds, and so on, which are not due to the external physical cause to which the unsophisticated savage refers them. In other words the visions do not result from the stimulation of the retina by light waves, nor are the sounds due to air waves falling upon the ear. The sensations are initiated in the organism, probably in the brain, though, if telepathy be a fact, we may in some cases have to look outside the organism for the ultimate source of the phenomenon.

A president of the Folklore Society once de-nounced the Society for Psychical Research, and all its ways, because it believed, or some of its members believed in spirits, his own view being that it was absolutely essential to the progress of science to exclude, once and for all, the deadly heresy of animism even when the human mind was the subject of inquiry. His ground for so doing was that savages believe in spirits; they attribute to the action of spirits many phenomena which men of science explain otherwise—consequently, spirits cannot exist.

A parallel argument will disprove the existence of horses. In the early days of the steam-engine a party of agricultural labourers stood gazing at one of the new and wonderful machines, and finally solved the puzzle by postulating a horse or horses in its interior, which made the wheels go round. Now Mr Clodd, if he be logical, will certainly admit that the conclusion to be drawn from this is, that horses do not exist.

(1) Savages explain many phenomena as due to spirits. (2) Many of these phenomena are *not* due to spirits. *Ergo*, spirits do not exist, he argues. (1) My labourers explain the action of a steam-engine as due to horses in its interior. (2) There was *no* horse in its interior. *Ergo*, horses do not exist.

The fact is, of course, that a mistaken explanation of one phenomenon does not invalidate the same explanation as applied to another phenomenon. If the Red Indian was mistaken in thinking that the aurora is due to the rubbing of the coats of celestial deer, an explanation at which he arrives by sound

reasoning from his premises, one of which—a fact
—was that earthly deer have coats which give
electric sparks under certain conditions, and the
other a hypothesis—or rather two hypotheses—
that there were deer in the sky, and that the coat
of a celestial deer alone could produce the results
which he saw, he is hardly superstitious.

Now Mr Clodd, whom we may take as our scientific Gallio, would say, and therein be supported
by the common consent of educated mankind, that
the animism of the savage is a superstition. I agree.
But is the savage explanation of the aurora a superstition too ? Perhaps it is, but there is no suggestion of a ghostly deer, and nothing occult about
this theory, any more than there is about the ether.

If this aurora theory is a superstition, how about
the horse theory of the steam-engine ? Here we
are dealing with everyday facts and objects; and
if Mr Clodd calls the labourers superstitious I do
not think common opinion will uphold him.

Let us assume, however, that he does. I go on
to ask if the chemist of a century ago was superstitious when he talked of phlogiston or regarded
heat as a substance. Here he was far more mythological than either the Red Indian or the labourers,
for no one now regards heat as a substance.

The man of science, to explain observed phenomena,
was postulating the existence of a non-existent
thing, which is just what the savage does when

he invokes a spirit to explain the motion of the sun or the howling of the wind.

The attempt to define superstition along these lines seems to lead, therefore, to an *impasse*. We fare no better, however, in other directions. It is useless to take the test of consensus of opinion ; for no such consensus exists as is required to constitute a valid argument, and, even if it did, there is no guarantee against either lack of knowledge or an epidemic of prejudice and want of common fairness and desire to get at the truth. The majority test is even less useful, for new ideas, or new renderings of old ideas, have always had to struggle against the forces of conservatism, which is too often only a name for lack of power to digest new facts and change one's views with the advance of knowledge.

A detailed examination of this question shows that the only definition of superstition which seems to meet all cases, even approximately, is that it implies in some way a departure from a norm. This is, however, equivalent to making it an entirely colourless epithet, for departure from a norm is by no means synonymous with error—one man's norm is another man's nonsense.

If, therefore, people really do see pictures in crystals the epithet of "superstitious" is meaningless. But how are we to prove that they do see pictures ?

Those who regard crystal gazing as a supersti-

tion are, of course, incredulous as to the visions said
to be seen in a crystal. Possibly if dreams were
as rare, relatively, as crystal visions are, they would
take up the same attitude with regard to dreams.

I recently discussed the question of crystal
gazing with one of the incredulous ones ; she
belonged to the sex whose privilege it is to be
absolutely illogical. Starting with the assertion
that she would not believe in crystal gazing unless
she could crystal-gaze herself, she maintained that
all experiences were to her incredible which she
had not experienced. Confronted with a concrete
example, she was fain to make an exception in favour
of drunkenness, and was thereafter ready to admit
the reality of crystal gazing if she could see a person
at the moment he or she was experiencing a crystal
vision, though what security this would give is not
quite clear.

It was pointed out to her that she had no guarantee
in such a case which she had not when the crystal
gazer signed a statement, and for the moment the
remark seemed to carry conviction. On the following day, as often happens, the old personal-experience
phase of conviction had reappeared, and the fair
sceptic would only admit the truth of a ghost story
(ghosts being then under discussion) if she could
see a ghost herself. This did not arise from any
mistrust of the veracity of ghost seers but from
an innate conviction of human liability to error,

a law to which, it appears, there was one exception.

The attitude just described is perhaps more pronounced, and more easily denounced, than that of the average man who does not believe " in all that nonsense," but it is hardly more illogical. In the case of ghosts and crystal visions, as of all other *prima facie* veridical * psychological experiences, there are two questions involved : (1) the personal experience of the seer, for which we must rely on his veracity; and (2) the agreement of this experience with unknown facts ; given a contemporary statement, or one so nearly contemporary as to anticipate the proof of the veridical nature of the scry, and the value of the record, so far as it concerns the supernormal character of the experience, is not readily assailed ; for errors, if any, are as likely to be in one direction as the other. Incredulity as to the fact of crystal gazing is synonymous with inexperience and with that lack of open-mindedness which is characterised by a refusal to investigate. Crystal gazing, I may say, for the benefit of blatant sceptics, is a recognised experiment even in orthodox psychological laboratories.

An amusing, if unimportant, objection is that

---

* By veridical is meant that the scryer or ghost seer has, through his vision, obtained information on points which do not lie within his normal sphere of knowledge—as, for example, the personal appearance of an actually unknown but identifiable person.

crystal gazing is of no use, the suggestion being that it is, consequently, non-existent. The same theory might be applied to dreams, but Mr Lang, as usual, has a story to show that crystal gazing on occasions, *is* useful. A friend of his declared that if winners could be spotted by it there would be some use in it ; his wife promptly " spotted " the winners of two races and, we may imagine, the husband became a convert on the spot. I hasten to add that I do not recommend this practice as a means of making money, nor does Mr Lang.

I forbear, however, to discuss the whole catalogue of objections to the practice of crystal gazing or to its reality, ranging from the belief that it is the work of the devil to the ready-made theory that all crystal gazers are neurotic and hysterical. A crystal vision is simply a day-dream. The faculty of crystal gazing is closely allied to that of visualising (or calling up the image of the object of which one is thinking), which is commonly found in young children (hence their use as scryers in mediæval times) and in artists. Those who doubt the allied faculty may be recommended to study Mr Francis Galton's " Inquiry into Human Faculty."

CHAPTER II

VISION AND VISIONS

"Real" things—"Unreal" things or hallucinations— Automatisms—After images—Mental pictures— Illusions hypnagogiques—Illusions proper— Reversible pictures

THE subject of vision and its varieties has already been dealt with in the volume on Thought Transference, apropos of the experiments in crystal gazing, but it will be necessary to consider the questions in greater detail here, where we are dealing specifically with visual impressions, whether " real " or otherwise. To the ordinary man who does not concern himself with metaphysical subtleties the things he sees are real when other people see them too, or when he himself can touch them or in some other way check the accuracy of the information supplied him by the sense of sight. It is true that we may suffer from hallucinations which affect two senses ; as we shall see later it is possible for a scryer (or crystal gazer) to see the lips of his vision people move and at the same time hear what they say; he thus suffers from both auditory and visual hallucinations.

9

Again, the test that more than one person sees a thing is apt to work out wrong in practice. Not only may two people see the same crystal vision (a case related by Mr Lang is very much to the point—two sceptics both saw an old lady, greatly to their disgust), but we need go no further than such a common failing as colour blindness to see that the test of common agreement may mean common agreement in a mistaken view of things ; for the perceptions of the colour blind are every bit as real to them as those of the normal sighted are to them ; and if we admit that half-a-dozen people are justified in regarding their perceptions as unquestionably real because they agree among themselves in their descriptions of what they see, half-a-dozen colour-blind people would be equally justified in regarding *their* sensations as normal because *they* agree. Now it so happens that in the case of colour blindness we can easily apply the test of common agreement at any time, and are thus in no doubt as to what is normal and " real," but in the case of crystal visions, and still more of the hallucinations commonly called ghosts, we can apply no such test.   On the theory of common agreement, therefore, ghosts and crystal visions must be reckoned as " real " if they pass the test of common agreement among those who were present and had an opportunity of seeing them—a view which does not commend itself.   Fortunately in the present chapter we are concerned rather with theoretical than with practical distinctions. We need not embark on a thorny discussion as to the "reality" of Blondlot's N-rays; nor need we consider what would be the result of a spread of colour blindness until only one half of the human race could see red as normal-sighted people see it to-day, while the other half denounced them as impostors for maintaining that there was anything except grey to be seen. All that we are here concerned to do is to point out that we do agree that our senses, working in what we call the normal way, tell us of certain things which we call real.

So far as the question immediately interesting us goes it is a byway, but it may be pointed out that, in a sense, the unfortunate engine-driver who brings a collision to pass owing to the fact that he cannot see a red lamp *red*, is, in a way, justified in calling his sensations real; for him his senses *are* working in their normal way; only, unluckily for him and the passengers, it does not happen to be the same way as that of the man who devised the signals. The real of the engine-driver is not the same as the real of the signalman; but we cannot say that either is hallucinated.

Unreal Things

This brings us to the definition of the term hallucination, which has for most people unpleasant associations of delirium tremens, hysteria, and diseased conditions. Let me assure them that as a term of psychology it has no such evil associations ; it may, of course, happen that the psychologist has to deal with a person suffering in the ways described, and then he is bound to speak of their perceptions as hallucinations. But in the ordinary course of things there is no suggestion of disease in the mind of the psychologist when he speaks of an hallucination ; all he means is that the person affected, whom we call the percipient, saw or heard or felt or smelt something just as if there were some external cause to produce this sensation, whatever it was, whereas, in fact, there was no external cause, the sensation being either an automatism or due to hypnotic suggestion.

The word automatism has an alarming look, but all it means is that what was seen or heard—or, to use a technical term, the percept—was due not to any external cause, nor yet to any intention on the part of the percipient (to this class of percepts we shall return in a moment), but, like Topsy, just " growed." There are two kinds of automatisms : called motor, or such as produce movement as in the case of the divining rod or automatic writing; and sensory, or such as cause our senses to deceive us as when we are dozing in the morning and seem to hear a knock—a very common experience with people who like an extra ten minutes before getting up.

The most familiar instance of an automatism is, however, a dream. A dream is only rarely, and then probably only to a very small extent, due to external causes; it is created by the activity of certain portions of the brain, in which the so-called higher centres seldom participate, with the result that our dreams are usually the most muddled performances imaginable, though it is only on reflection that we realise this, just as it is only on reflection that we discover that hallucinations of our waking moments *are* hallucinations and not ordinary waking percepts. It will probably serve to dispel any unpleasant taste still remaining after the word hallucination if we remark that the best hallucinations, and almost the only pure type, are dreams, which are so common as to be regarded as absolutely normal in most people, though there are others who never dream (or at any rate never recall that they have dreamt) and others again, among whom is myself, who dream perhaps not more than a dozen times a year, but on these rare occasions with great vividness.

After Images

Between the ordinary sense perceptions of normal persons and pure hallucinations, such as dreams, which are absolutely individual in their character (I leave out of the question telepathic dreams, as involving needless elaboration of points which are for our present purpose unimportant), there are many intermediate stages, some of which are neither ordinary sense perceptions nor yet hallucinations.

In the first place we have after images. Everyone is familiar with the fact that after looking at a bright light certain sensations persist, or rather run through a series of changes, long after the original object has ceased to stimulate the optic nerve. If one lies on one's back on the deck of a ship and looks at the rigging against the bright summer sky, and then closes one's eyes, the resulting after images are remarkably vivid and enduring, and the colours thus presented to us are often of exceeding beauty. In my own case they endure for fully two minutes after I have closed my eyes, and represent, in the earlier stages, the ropes of the rigging, at which I have been looking ; then the various lines gradually fuse together, until only a mass of colour remains, which gradually fades away.

Sometimes our after images will give us information which the original sensation has denied us.

If I walk up Tottenham Court Road in the evening, and look at the brilliant electric lights outside the Oxford Music Hall, I fail to see the word " Oxford " on the globe—the illumination is excessive—but if I close my eyes (turning them away usually fails to produce the same effect) I see quite distinctly the word Oxford, or, at any rate, some of the letters come out in black on a white ground ; this after image disappears without going through any series of colour changes, so far as I have been able to see —a result possibly due to the difference of conditions. For in the street it is difficult to lie down and observe the changes without attracting some attention, and possibly receiving an invitation to accompany a gentleman in blue.

These after images may also be postponed, and appear several hours after the original stimulations of the optic nerve. Cases are on record where people have looked at a candle just before closing the eyes at night, and then seen the after image of it for a moment immediately after opening the eyes the following morning.*

Mental Pictures

As a rule, however, it is safe to say that mental pictures, as they are termed, seen after such a long interval are memory images, not direct results of

* *Proc. S.P.R.* viii. 450.

the stimulation of the retina. How, it may be
asked, does a mental image differ from a hallucination ? A hallucination, as we have seen, is an
affection of the senses, which seems at first sight
to be caused by some external object ; to use a
technical expression, it is externalised ; it seems
to be wholly outside us, whereas mental images and
some intermediate phenomena can be seen with
closed eyes, or are at any rate independent of the
external world, or take no place among the surroundings of the percipient, as is the case with
hallucinations proper.

Many people are able to recall in the form of a
memory image any well-known scene, or even scenes,
which they have visited but once and almost forgotten (here we verge on the " automatism)."
Others, among whom I am numbered, are unable, or
but very rarely able, to call up a picture, and their
pictures are far less vivid than the reality. This
faculty of picturing to one's mind's eye is termed
visualising. Good visualisers are able not only to
recall scenes that have been present before their
eyes of the flesh, but to construct pictures of their
own, exactly as dreamers automatically construct
the scenery of their dreams.

"ILLUSIONS HYPNAGOGIQUES" AND THEIR ALLIES

Another class of perceptions are called pseudo-hallucinations. They are unlike the memory and fancy images of which we have just been speaking in being more steady, as well as in being spontaneous; they are, in fact, what are termed automatisms. They differ from the full-blown hallucination in not forming a part of the ordinary surroundings of the seer. Thus, one lady describes such scenes as being, as it were, enclosed in a sort of soap bubble, which seemed to come sailing into the room on a beam of light. She was quite aware that these visions were unreal, and could see them with closed eyes equally well. They were not the result of disease, for she states that they were vivid when she was in good health, and *vice versa*.

The most common form of these pseudo-hallucinations is what is often termed "faces in the dark," the technical term for which is hypnagogic illusions. Many sane and healthy people have, in the interval between sleeping and waking, mental images of surprising vividness. Judging by the only occasion on which I have experienced anything of this sort they are fully as distinct as objects seen in the normal way under a bright light.

Faces are not the only objects, of course; they may be scenes, known or unknown, or, as in my own

B

case, something fantastic; what I saw was a long procession of eyes—lions' eyes, crocodiles' eyes, snakes' eyes, all sorts of eyes—and that in a state of perfect health, so far as I could judge.

Often some connection may be traced between these pictures and the thoughts of the percipient. Thus, one percipient had been reading of Brynhilda, and lay in bed thinking about her life, when " out there came in the darkness a grand face—worth anyone's toil to transfer it to canvas—and so vivid that, years after, he could have depicted it if he had been an artist." It may be noted in passing that the artist seldom succeeds in transferring to canvas with full satisfaction to himself the pictures which he has seen in his mind's eye.

With the *illusion hypnagogique* we reach the verge of the hallucination proper; and it is, in fact, a matter of no small difficulty to discriminate between some forms of them and the full-blown hallucination. We are, however, not concerned with these questions here, the crystal visions being clearly of the type of the soap-bubble vision already mentioned. We shall deal with them more in detail in the next chapter.

ILLUSION

Up to the present we have been dealing either with pictures entirely divorced from the objects of the surrounding world or with those entirely dependent on •them (leaving out of account such matters as the element of experience in our judgments of distance and similar points). We now come to a class of percepts which agree with the mistaken sensations of the colour blind in being other than they seem to be and in being due to external objects, but differ from them in being, like hallucinations, recognisable as erroneous, at any rate in most cases, as soon as we turn our attention to them. These are termed illusions. They are mal-interpretations of stimuli received from the external world, and worked up by our minds into a picture, which often bears very little relation to the real thing before us.

As an example we may take a case from the Census of Hallucinations,* the percipient being Professor Sorley, now of Cambridge.

" Lying in bed," he says, " and opening my eyes voluntarily in order to drive away the imagery of an unpleasant dream, which was beginning to revive, I saw the figure of a man, some three or four feet distant from my head, standing perfectly still by the bedside, so close to it that the bedclothes seemed slightly pushed towards me by his leg pressing against them. The image was perfectly distinct, height about five feet eight inches, sallow complexion, grey eyes, greyish moustache, short and bristly, and apparently recently clipped. His dress seemed like a dark grey dressing-gown, tied with a dark red rope.

" My first thought was ' that's a ghost ' ; my second ' it may be a burglar, whose designs upon my watch are interrupted by my opening my eyes.' I bent forward towards him, and the image vanished. As it vanished, my attention passed to a

* *Proc. S.P.R.* x. 94.

shadow on the wall twice or three times the distance off, and perhaps twelve feet high.   There was a gas lamp in the lane outside which shed a light through the lower twelve inches or so of the window, . . . and the shadow was caused by the curtain hanging beside the window.   The solitary bit of colour in the image—the red rope in the dressing-gown—was immediately after identified as the twisted red mahogany handle of the dressing table, which was in the same line of vision as part of the shadow."

Professor Sorley remarks that this illusion has no connection with the dream, which he also mentions ; otherwise one would be tempted to regard it as simply a survival from the dream projected into the surrounding portion of the external world. Once, on waking from a dream, in which an omnibus figured, with the words " Baker Street to ——" on the side, in vexation at not being able to discover whether it was the one I wanted (my subliminal had not been equal to the creation of a 'bus conductor, nor had it occurred to me to ask the driver), I thought to myself : " Bother that 'bus ; if I look again I may see it somewhere else."   So I opened my eyes, and on the wall just before me the word " Waterloo," in large letters, developed, and persisted for some ten seconds.

There is another class of illusions, which, however, hardly concerns us here (the bearing of illusions on crystal visions will be seen in the next chapter). These are the familiar experiences with puzzle pictures, in which a face or figure has to be found, and which, to myself, are usually *introuvable* ; or, in a more complex form, the reversible pictures, of which many examples are now sold, such as the duck-rabbit, or the pile of cubes. Having seen the picture one way, it is only by a considerable effort that we are able to reverse it. Properly speaking, these interchangeable effects can hardly be included among illusions, inasmuch as both effects are equally real, and can be reproduced at will, which is not the case with an illusion proper.

CHAPTER III

CRYSTAL VISIONS

*Genesis of visions—Ibn Kaldoun on crystal gazing—
Modern descriptions—Miss Angus—Optical laws
of visions*

TURNING now to crystal visions in particular, we
may, from a theoretical point of view, divide them
into two main classes, the line of demarcation between which is the same as that between hallucinations and illusions, though in other respects the
two classes of crystal visions do not belong to either
of these categories, being, as we have already seen,
pseudo-hallucinations, or objects apparently external but not forming in any real sense part of the
outside world. The class of crystal visions which
is on all-fours with pure hallucinations is that which
is seen (and it may be noted that we use crystal
vision as a convenient general term for any vision
depending for its genesis on practices described in
Chapters V. and VI.) in perfectly dark objects. A
friend of Mr Lang's, for example, made his first experiment by looking into a perfectly dark funnel, covering
up his head so as to exclude all sources of illumination except internal ones. He soon found that

the funnel filled with light, and then fancy pictures followed. Singularly enough, this experimenter does not recall a single dream, and, if we may assume that his non-recollection is a proof of non-existence, never does dream.

In other cases, and these approach illusions very closely sometimes, the crystal picture originates in the small specks of light or shade or colour which are found in every crystal (these are termed in technical language *points de repère*); or may, like an illusion proper, be manufactured out of reflections and shadows in the crystal; but, once initiated, seem to be independent of them, and in this respect are, of course, sharply distinguished from illusions of the ordinary type.

In the case of good scryers the crystal picture seems to develop instantaneously. Mr Lang records the case of a girl who picked up the ball, and saw in it a piece of paper covered with writing which she took to be in the ball. Another actually turned the ball round, expecting to see the picture on the back.

In other cases the ball seems to fill with mist, and perhaps ends by disappearing; or the mist may clear away, and the picture be seen, as it would be if a curtain were drawn away. On this point the observations of Ibn Kaldoun are of interest:

Ceux qui regardent dans les corps diaphanes

tels que les miroirs, les cuvettes remplies d'eau et les liquides ; ceux qui inspectent les cœurs, les foies et les os des animaux ; ceux qui prédisent par le jet de cailloux ou de noyaux, tous ces gens-là appartiennent à la catégorie des devins. . . . Ils tachent d'arriver au but en essayant de concentrer en un seul sens toutes leurs perceptions. Comme la vue est le sens le plus noble, ils lui donnent la préférence, fixant leurs régards sur un objet à superficie unie, ils le considèrent avec attention jusqu'à ce qu'ils y aperçoivent la chose qu'ils veulent annoncer. Quelques personnes croient que l'image aperçue de cette manière se dessine sur la surface du miroir ; mais ils se trompent. Le devin regarde fixement cette surface jusqu'à ce qu'elle disparaisse et qu'un rideau, semblable à un brouillard s'interpose entre lui et le miroir. Sur ce rideau se dessinent les formes qu'il desire aperçevoir et cela lui permet de donner des indications, soit affirmatives, soit négatives, sur ce qu'on désire savoir. Il raconte alors les perceptions tels qu'il les reçoit. Les devins pendant qu'ils sont dans cet état, n'aperçoivent pas ce qui se voit réellement (dans le miroir) ; c'est un autre mode de perception qui naît chez eux et qui s'opère, non pas au moyen de la vue, mais de l'âme. Il est vrai que, pour eux, les perceptions de l'âme ressemblent à celles des sens au point de les tromper ; fait qui, du reste, est bien connu. La même chose arrive à ceux qui examinent les cœurs et les foies d'animaux [ou qui regardent dans l'eau, dans les cuvettes ou dans d'autres objets du même genre].* Nous avons vu quelques-uns de ces individus entraver l'opération des sens par l'emploi de simples fumigations ; puis se servir d'incantations afin de donner à l'âme la disposition requise ; ensuite ils racontent ce qu'ils ont aperçu. Ces formes, disent-ils, se montrent dans l'air et représentent des personnages ; elles leur apprennent, au moyen d'emblèmes et de signes, les choses qu'ils cherchent à savoir. Les individus de cette classe se détachent moins de l'influence des sens que ceux de la classe précédente. L'univers est plein de merveilles.†

On a later page the author remarks : ‡

Les gens qui se servent de pareilles procédés avec l'intention de connaître les secrets du monde invisible ne font et ne disent rien qui vaille.

Another scryer describes her experiences as follows :—

I soon see a pale golden light, seemingly uniting,

* This passage appears to be a later addition.

† IBN KALDOUN, in *Notices et Extraits des MSS. de la Bibl. Imp.* xix. 221. Ibn Kaldoun was born at Tunis in 1332. He was in the service of various sultans, and at the age of thirty went to Spain. He led a wandering life, and wrote his *Prolegomena.* from which this extract is taken, about 1374, in an Algerian town called Taoughzout.

‡ *Ibid.* p. 240

frequently cut with flashes of electric or magnetic light. In the soft, pale, golden light there appears a spot of deep yellow gold moving about, sometimes in a circle. After watching it for some time it resolves itself into something like an eye, with a dark, deep blue pupil; then with a ring of gold around the eye centre; then into a ring of lighter blue, resembling an eye. I first saw this object two or three weeks after purchasing the mirror. The first object I saw at all was in the evening, when I was sitting with back towards the bright lamplight. I had sat about twenty minutes, impatient and discouraged at seeing nothing but a black mirror, when suddenly the appearance described above showed itself near the left-hand lower corner of the disc, slowly passing upward two-thirds the way towards the right-hand upper corner, when it suddenly disappeared. This has been repeated several times with variations. Its size is that of a silver dime.*

[*R. goes on*]—I know cases where that identical spot of golden light has resolved itself into an ethereal lane, through which magnificent supernal realities have been seen. . . . More than this, I have known three persons at one time, in broad daylight, see the same thing — a magnificent living picture embodying the most splendid arabesque scenery.

According to Miss Angus the vision sometimes

* Randolph, *Seership*, p. 74.

appears small and far away—deep in the glass, as it were. At other times the glass seems to disappear, as described by Ibn Kaldoun; but Miss Angus seems to think that this disappearance is preceded by the emergence of the vision. As soon as she tries to analyse the picture or her sensations the whole scene vanishes.*

The pictures, she says, are by no means stationary. Illustrative cases will be found in some of Mr Lang's narratives; and it is particularly striking that a whole mass of minute detail is grasped in a momentary flash, for her pictures, like our dreams probably, seem to be very fleeting. Sometimes, but this may be a hallucinatory memory, she believes that she can recall fresh details an hour or two after the picture has gone. The only test of such an occurrence would be for her to give veridical details of something at a distance. In itself, of course, the thing is by no means improbable; to a less extent the same phenomenon is observable in after images.†

While she is describing the first vision Miss Angus frequently finds that a second, which is related to the first in some way, appears.

Mrs Verrall does not say how the pictures come into existence; but her remarks are of considerable

* *Jl.* viii. 222 *et seq.* For some of Miss Angus's scries see p. 142 below.

† For other descriptions see *Proc. S.P.R.* viii. 499 *et seq.*

interest, and may be quoted here. She is a good visualiser, and has no difficulty in calling up a mental picture; but the visions seen on looking into a crystal or glass of water are, she says, in some respects unlike all other visual impressions. A dim light is, in her case, most effectual; but she has seen the pictures in bright light too—never, however, like Mr Lang's friend, in absolute darkness. For Mrs Verrall the picture is built up from the bright points in the crystal, but, once produced, the picture has a reality which she cannot give to her mental images. She has seldom been able to investigate the effect of a magnifying-glass on her visions, as they always temporarily disappeared. In some cases, however, they remained unaffected, and in one case a temporary enlargement took place, though this was not the normal effect of the lens. I do not know whether Mrs Verrall is very suggestible, nor yet, if she is, what her expectations were in the case of enlargement. The phenomenon suggests that optical laws had nothing to do with the case.*

Crystal visions are equally unaffected in other cases by the use of optical instruments. A friend of Mr Andrew Lang gets crystal pictures, but they are unaffected by wearing spectacles. He, however, saw his visions more distinctly than real

* *Proc. S.P.R.* viii. 473. See also *Proc. S.P.R.* viii. 486, 500.

objects. In this connection it is of interest to note that the pictures presented by mirage in the desert are said to be rendered more distinct by the use of a field-glass. The gentleman in question saw a face on one occasion, and on turning the glass saw it in profile.*

In some cases, however, experiments seem to show that the use of magnifying-glasses and other optical instruments may modify the crystal picture. A well-known optician of Bond Street carried out a series of experiments with Miss Goodrich-Freer some years ago, and arranged the conditions so that she could not be aware of the normal effects of the four lenses employed on real objects. Suggestion was thus avoided.† In all, eight experiments were tried, and in five the pictures behaved like a real object. The lenses were fitted into four pairs of eyeglasses, and their respective effects on real objects at the given distance would have been : *A* to duplicate the object vertically ; *B* to blur it ; *C* no effect ; *D* to duplicate it horizontally. The experimenter, Mr Dixey, handed the lenses personally to Miss Freer, and the experiments resulted as follows :—

(1) *A* gave distance.

(2) *B* picture disappeared, then became more intense.

* *Jl. S.P.R.* viii. 222.   † *Proc. S.P.R.* x. 108.

(3) Picture disappeared.

In all these cases no such effect would have been produced on real objects. In two cases, 6 and 7, the result would have been attained in looking at real objects if the right eye alone had been used ; they were :

(6) *A* lowered part of the picture.

(7) *D* moved it to the right.

In the other cases the *A*, *C*, and *D* glasses had their normal effect. How far this difference of results between Mrs Verrall's experiment, carried out under the same conditions, and Miss Freer's is attributable to a difference in the type of their hallucinations it is difficult to say. *A priori*, it might be expected that Mrs Verrall, who uses, and knows that she uses, *points de repère*, would be the one to find that her pictures behaved like real objects ; while Miss Goodrich-Freer, whose pictures are as spontaneous as Mrs Verrall's, and not preceded by any mist or curtain in the crystal, should find her visions unaffected—unless, indeed, her omission to notice the influence of *points de repère* * does not mean that *points de repère* play no part, or only a very small part, in the development of her visions. The point is an interesting one, and if

* *Proc. S.P.R.* vi. 485.

any crystal gazer who reads these lines will try some experiments and communicate them to me I shall be very glad. Of especial interest would it be to know what happens in the case of those persons whose visions are preceded by the disappearance of the crystal.

CHAPTER IV

THE SPECULUM, AND THE METHOD OF USING IT

Tritheim's recipe—Paracelsus—Dr Dee—Magical and religious recipes—Modern mysteries—Advice of practical scryers

IN the following chapters we shall see that a great variety of objects are used to promote the externalisation of subliminal images. Not only is the plain crystal, or its congener the black stone, used, together with its first cousin the mirror, and the primitive substitute of water, but almost any bright object seems to have been employed at one time or another. Thus we find the sword among the Romans; and in mediæval Europe polished iron is suggested in Faust's *Höllenzwang*; lamp-black is sometimes smeared on the hand, or, as we shall see later, a pool of ink poured into it; visions are seen in smoke and flame, in black boxes, in jugs, and on white paper; in more than one place we find that diviners gaze at the livers of slain animals to provoke hallucinations; and a classical and mediæval method, which has lasted until our own day, consisted in blindfolding the seer, and suggesting to him that he should scry in a mirror with the top of his head.

PLATE I.]

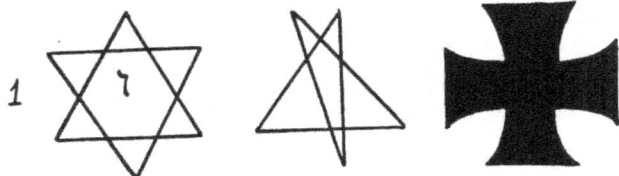

1

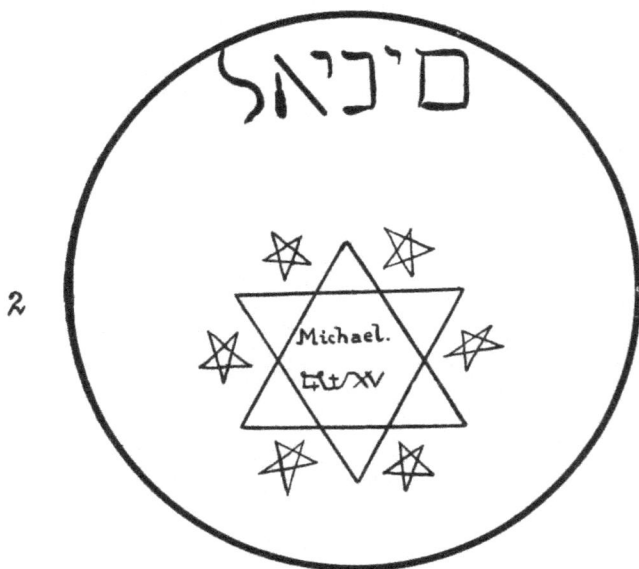

2

In the idea of mediæval scryers, however, the selection of a speculum was no light matter, to be undertaken without due preparation, as we shall presently see in the quotations from the *Höllenzwang*.

For the preparation of the speculum, shew-stone, symph, or triune there are many recipes. Here are some of them :

The Abbot Tritheim says : " Procure of a lapidary a good, clear, pellucid crystal of the bigness of a small orange—*i.e.* about one inch and a half in diameter ; let it be globular, or round each way alike ; then, when you have got this crystal fair and clear, without any clouds or specks, get a small plate of fine gold to encompass the crystal round one half ; let this be fitted on an ivory or ebony pedestal. Let there be engraved a circle round the crystal, with these characters around inside the circle next the crystal. (*See* Plate I., figure 1.) Afterwards the name Tetragrammaton. On the other side of the plate let there be engraven : ' Michael, Gabriel, Uriel, Raphael,' which are the four principal angels ruling over the Sun, Moon, Venus, and Mercury. The table on which the crystal stands must be inscribed as shown in Plate I., figure 2.*

Paracelsus recommends you to take ten parts of pure gold, ten of silver, five of copper, two of tin, two of lead, one of iron-filings, and five of mercury.

* *Trith.* in Barrett, *Magus,* 135.

C

Melt the lead and add the mercury when Saturn and Mercury are in conjunction. Let it cool, and reheat it when Jupiter is in conjunction with the two already named, and add the tin. When one of these planets is in conjunction with the Sun, the Moon, or Venus, add the gold, silver, and copper. Then at a conjunction with Mars add the powdered iron. Stir with a dry witch-hazel.

Your mirror should have a diameter of two inches, and should be cast in sand at a conjunction of Jupiter and Venus. Smooth it with a grindstone, and polish with tripoly and a piece of limewood, when the planetary influences are favourable. When the mirror is prepared keep it in a clean linen cloth, and you may see in it the past and the present, and all the doings of men, all that has ever been spoken or written, and the person who said it, and his reasons.

One account of Dr Dee's speculum is that it was a flat black stone of very close texture, with a highly-polished surface, half-an-inch in thickness, and seven and a quarter in diameter; of a circular form, except at the top, where there is a sort of loop, with a hole for suspension.* Horace Walpole put the following note on the back:—

The black stone into which Dr Dee used to call his spirits, *v.* his book. This stone was men-

* *N. and Q.* iv. 155.

tioned in the catalogue of the collection of the Mordaunts, Earls of Peterborough, passed into the hands of Lady Elizabeth Germaine, from whom it went to John Campbell, Duke of Argyll, whose son, Lord Frederick Campbell, presented it to H. W.

At the Strawberry Hill sale it was purchased by Mr Smythe Piggott, and at his sale in 1853 was purchased by Lord Londesborough.

At the Tudor Exhibition in 1890 two magic mirrors were on view—one a real crystal, lent by G. Milner-Gibson-Cullum, the other a pear-shaped polished black stone. Probably the real fact of the matter is that Dr Dee had more than one " speculum."

A rock-crystal ball is shown in the British Museum as Dr Dee's " shew-stone," but there is no reason to suppose that it is genuine. There are also, it may be mentioned, two crystals from a Saxon cemetery in the Isle of Wight, one dull, the other polished; both are enclosed in two metal bands, with means for suspending them. An analogous crystal, from Shetland, was recently shown at the Folklore Society, and there stated to be, according to tradition, of Oriental origin. Other examples are in the Dublin Museum.

In some cases magic was practised in order to ensure the efficacy of the crystal.

A MS. in the Ashmolean says : " First get a

broad square crystall or Venice Glasse, in length 8, breadth 3 inches. Then lay that glasse or crystall in the bloud of a white henne 3 Wednesdayes or 3 Fridayes. Then take it out and wash it with holy aq. and fumigate it. Then take 3 Hazle sticks or wands of an year growth, peel them fayre and white ; and make them so long as you can write the spiritt's name or fayrie's which you call, 3 times on every stick being made flatt on one side. Then bury them under some Hill, whereas ye suppose the fayries haunt, the Wed. before you call her, and the Friday following take them uppe and call her at 8 or 3 or 10 o'clock, when be good planetts and houres for that time but when you call turn thy face towards the East. And when you have her bind her to that stone or glasse.

"For myself I call Margaret Barence, but this will obtain any one that is not already bound."

In other cases a religious element comes in. Aubrey says of a crystal: "This beryl is a perfect sphere, the diameter of which I guess to be something more than an inch ; it is set in a ring or circle of silver resembling the meridian of a globe ; the stem of it is about ten inches high, all gilt. At the four quarters of it are the names of four angels—viz. Uriel, Raphael, Michael, Gabriel. On the top is a cross patee." (*See* Plate II.)

Of another he says : "A beryl in the possession of Sir Edward Harley, Knight of the Bath, which he

PLATE II.]

keeps in his closet at Brampton-Bryan, in Hereford-
shire, amongst his Cimelia, came first from Norfolk.
A minister had it there, and a call was to be used
with it. Afterwards a miller had it, and both did
work great cures with it (if curable), and in the beryl
they did see either the receipt in writing or else the
herb. To this minister the spirits or angels would
appear openly; and because the miller, who was his
familiar friend, one day happened to see them he
gave him the aforesaid beryl and call. By these
angels the minister was forewarned of death.
Afterwards this beryl came into somebody's hand
in London, who did tell strange things by it, inso-
much that at last he was questioned for it, and it
was taken away by authority [about 1645]." *

Modern spiritualists or mystics have precepts for
the use of crystals.

A modern author says the mirror must be an
oblate spheroid with two foci, so that the magical
fluids slide along the surface from one to other. It
must be concave, otherwise the fluid would bound
off or collect underneath. It must be made of a thin
film of gold; then a compound of fifteen bodies,
associated with phthallic acid and paranaphthalene
(these are elective and electric), and so on.† I will
not inflict a full description on my readers.

"These are dear," says the author. "A cheap

* Aubrey, *Miscellanies*, iv. 219.
† Randolph, *Seership*, p. 55.

substitute is the following :—Mould a lump of clay *slightly convex*. Dry, bake it hard, and smooth its surface ; then press pasteboard till all is smooth and even. Now make a concave one to match ; sheet of fine plate-glass between ; bake till it shapes itself. Make two alike ; between these two cemented pour black ink till full ; seal the aperture."

The same fanciful author says * there are three sorts of crystals :

(1) Mule or neuter : this is small.

(2) Well-sexed or female : the foci are true ; it is very sensitive.

> Abdul Aziz had one of a diamond (value £80,000) on the back of his watch. Maharajah Dhuleep Singh had a diamond, a ruby, and an emerald.

(3) Male mirror : the foci four inches apart.

The mirror is only to be handled by its owner, or the magnetisms will be mixed ; others may look at it in a box.

Clean it with soapsuds, rinse well, wash with alcohol or fluoric acid, and polish with velvet.

It must be frequently magnetised—make passes with the right hand, five ' at a time. This keeps it *alive*. If you make them with the left hand it gives it sensitiveness.

* Randolph, *Seership*, p. 87.

Have your back to the light *always*.

The top must lean from the scryer.

When several look it must be suspended.

You will see clouds first—they are really on the " magnetic field," which collects from the eyes of the scryer. Persons of a magnetic temperament— brunette, dark-eyed, brown-skinned—charge it quicker, but not more effectually, than blondes, who are of an electric temperament.

Never expose the mirror to direct sunlight. The visions seen in the left hand are real ; those in the right hand are symbolic. Ascending clouds mean Yes ; descending clouds mean No.

Those who like to carry out Mr Randolph's directions will give themselves a good deal of trouble to no purpose. The only useful suggestion which he makes is that the back should be to the light—a condition on which most crystal gazers of my acquaintance insist. On the other hand, I have heard of a scryer who looked at a candle flame through an egg-shaped crystal, and got equally good results.

Mr Lang makes the following suggestions :— It is best to go alone into a room, sit down with the back to the light, place the ball on the lap, at a just focus, on a dark dress or dark piece of cloth ; try to exclude reflections, think of anything you please, and stare for, say, five minutes at the ball. If after two or three trials you see nothing in the ball (which may seem to vanish, leaving only the pictures) you will probably never succeed.

If the experience of the Indian Mussulman goes for anything, I rather suspect Mr Lang has cut his period of probation rather short. As we have seen in the Qanoon-e-Islam, they recommend the scryer to go on for three quarters of an hour or more. Again, two or three trials are certainly too few. Even in the case of a specially-gifted scryer the power is often absent for weeks at a time, just as in other cases dreams sometimes come in shoals, and then fail to put in an appearance, or at anyrate to leave any impression on the waking consciousness, for months at a time. I have, personally, never seen anything, so my own advice does not go for much ; but I suspect Mr Lang is in the same case. I should try, if I did not already know that I am no scryer, for ten minutes or more ; in fact, till the eyes got tired. I should make two or three trials at a time, in the afternoon or early evening by preference, at intervals of ten days or a fortnight, and only after several sets should I give up the attempt.

Miss Goodrich-Freer's experience may be of value to good visualisers. I, therefore, give her suggestions here :

Look carefully at some part of the room in front of you, avoiding anything likely to be reflected in the ball. Shut your eyes, and try to visualise it ;

then try if you can see it in the crystal. If you have any gift of visualisation at all this ought to be acquired with ease after half-a-dozen experiments.

When you can do this you may go on to visualise, with closed eyes, some scene that you have lately witnessed—and this, too, can be transferred to the crystal. It is well to begin with simple subjects, and increase their complexity *pari passu* with the growth of your powers. Begin, say, with a chair— the only thing that I have ever been able to visualise at will, so far as my memory serves me; then take more complex objects; then try a simple scene, with one person and a background, and so on.

CHAPTER V

HISTORICAL

Savage scryers—Crystal gazing in initiation ceremonies—Crystal gazing in India, China, Persia —The mirror of Pythagoras

ALL the world over man seems to have discovered that pictures or visions can be seen in a speculum or some clear depth, and naturally uses it, as is the case with no small section of society in our own day, for the purpose of discovering the future, or trying to do so, or of finding out what is going on at a distance. With their success or otherwise we are not concerned in this chapter, which is simply an account of the various methods in vogue. A correspondent of Mr Andrew Lang's states that in West Australia the *boylya* or medicine man " puts himself into the crystal " to descry the results of a distant expedition. It is probably a common practice; for the crystal is a valuable part of the medicine man's equipment all over Australia, so much so that women are not allowed to look at it ; he uses it for rain-making and, in the state of fragments, for curing diseases. In West Australia the scryer, apparently, sometimes uses the flame of the burial fire.* In New Zealand the more civilised Maori use a drop of blood for their speculum. The custom probably exists among other Polynesian peoples; but the only mention of it known to me is a case given by Ellis among the Fijians, a people of Melanesian type and Polynesian customs. When goods had been stolen a priest looked in a hole dug in the floor of the house and filled with water. The belief was that a god brought the image of the thief over the water, in which it is reflected.

In South America the Huilli-che treasure-seekers look earnestly for the object of their search into a smooth slab of black stone.† Captain Bourke found a crystal-gazing jossakeed among the Apaches of the west of the United States; and Lejeune describes how the Red Indian doctors made their patients prescribe for themselves by the simple method of gazing into water, wherein they saw pictures of the things that would do them good—a simple method of enlisting the powers of suggestion, which may be commended to modern hypnotic doctors, and one which, besides, supplies them with an excellent excuse if the patient, as sometimes happens, fails to profit by his visit to the leech.

The Pawnees of the west of the United States seem to have had something akin to crystal gazing.

* Grey, *Journals,* ii. 346.
† References not given here will be found in Lang, *Making of Religion.*

When a badger was killed it was kept by the older people till night, and then skinned. The blood was poured into a bowl, and the children had to look at themselves in it by moonlight. If they saw themselves with grey hair it meant long life ; if the picture was dark and indistinct the child would die of sickness ; if no picture were seen at all the child would live, and be killed by the enemy.* The account is not very clear, but seems obviously to relate to viscous and not ordinary reflections.

Among the Iroquois the crystal was placed in a gourd of water to render visible the apparition of a person who has bewitched another, exactly as they do in the Hebrides to this day.†

In Yucatan the main instrument of the diviner is the zaztun (the clear stone), a quartz crystal or similar object, before which he burns gum copal as an incense, and recites magic formulas in an archaic dialect. This done, the stone has the power of reflecting the past and the future. The soothsayer gazes into its clear depths, and sees where lost articles are reposing, learns what is happening to the absent, and by whose witchery sickness and disaster have descended upon those who have called him in to their aid. It is said that nearly every village in Yucatan has one of these stones.

In Mexico crystal gazing seems to have been

---

* *Mem. Am. Folklore S.* viii. 351
† Brinton, *Essays*, p. 165.

known,* and in Peru one of the Incas is said to have discovered crystal gazing.

In Sarawak the manang or shaman uses Batu ilan or Batu enggan meda samengat, quartz crystals (specimens are to be seen in the Pitt Rivers Museum, Oxford), to view the condition of his patient's soul, which may be seen in the " sight stone " mingled with the souls of the well, or separated from them, the latter condition being the most serious. After finding the soul in the " stone of light " the manang goes into a trance ; when he wakes he has the soul of the sick man in his hand, in the shape of a bit of wood, or, it may be, a small beetle—thus going one better than Scheffer's Finnish shaman, who only brought back inanimate tokens from the foreign lands he visited.†

Sir Frank Swettenham found an Arab in the Malay Peninsula whose methods seem to be much the same as those of the Egyptian magicians and Indian Mohammedans. Having lost some property, he was advised by several Malay friends to go to a diviner. He had not much faith in the method, but, being a man of open mind, who recognises that phenomena may be seen, especially in the East, which are not explained by modern text-books on natural philosophy, he made the trial.

* *Archiv. f. Anth.*, N.S. ii. 45.
† *J. Anth. Inst.* xxxiii. ; *cf.* Ling Roth, *Natives of Sarawak*, i. 273 *et seq.*

The first diviner was " an Arab of very remarkable appearance. He was about fifty years old,
tall, with pleasant features and extraordinary grey-
blue eyes, clear and far-seeing, a man of striking and
impressive personality. . . . He said he would be
able to tell me all about the robbery, who committed it, where the stolen property then was, and
that all he would want was an empty house wherein
he might fast in solitude for three days, without
which preparation, he said, he would not be able to
see what he sought. He told me that, after his
vigil, fast, and prayer, he would lay on his hand a
small piece of paper on which there would be some
writing ; into this he would pour a little water, and
in this extemporised mirror he would see a vision
of the whole transaction. He declared that, after
gazing intently into this divining-glass, the inquirer
first recognised the figure of a little old man. Then,
having duly saluted this *jin*, it was necessary to
ask him to conjure up the scene of the robbery,
when all the details would be re-enacted in the
liquid glass under the eyes of the gazer, who
would there and then describe all he saw. I
had heard all this before, only it had been stated
to me that the medium through whose eyes
the vision could alone be seen must be a young
child of such tender years that it could never
have told a lie ! The Arab, however, professed
himself not only able to conjure up the scene,

but to let me see it for myself if I would follow his directions."*

Unfortunately, Sir Frank was travelling when he met this diviner, and they never met again. A local chief professed to have the power ; but his medium apparently became cataleptic as soon as the vision began to develop, and was not restored for two hours. "After that all the mothers of tender-aged and possibly truthful children," says Sir Frank, " declined to lend their children." The chief was not at the end of his resources, and a trial with a divining-bowl, which moved in the hands of the holder when a piece of paper containing the name of the thief was placed on the top, was completely successful. Mr Skeat † informs me that more than one other method of gazing is in use among the Malays. I have mentioned that in Australia the smoke and flame of the burial fire seem to be used for divination. In Malacca they use the flame of a candle for gazing, and profess to see visions in it. Unfortunately, I have no details as to the procedure or results.

Another method is to chew betel, and use the coloured saliva, in a metal cup or other vessel, as a speculum.

In Japan black boxes are said to be used, ‡ and

* Skeat, *Malay Magic*, 538.
† MS. note.
‡ MS. note.

in Siberia and East Russia the shamans look into the vessel.*

In the notes to the 1888 edition of the Chinese criminal code we find the following details as to crystal gazing in China:—It is known as Yüan-kuang-fuchou, the magic of the round glittering, and was practised by a certain Sun-yuang-sheng. When anything was lost he used to hang up a piece of white paper, and utter a spell, having at the same time a strip of paper with magic formulæ. Then he made a boy look at the paper, and he, without any picture on the paper before him, described the face and clothes of the thief. The magician, in accordance with the law against imposture, was punished for using spells. The Yüan-kuang-fuchou is very common in Pekin, and the authorities take no steps to hinder the traffic. A story is told of a European who lost a valuable photographic lens, and recovered it by the aid of a medium, he himself being the scryer. Possibly a shrewd suspicion of the thief, and his identity—he was an official well known to the scryer—helped the development of the hallucination.

Other methods of discovering the thief are the more familiar ones of the bowl of clean water, and the mirror.†

The Indian Mohammedans ‡ use " viewing of unjun (lamp-black) or the magic mirror."

* *Mitt., Ges. Ost. Asiens*, vi. 28.
† *Cf.* Du Halde, *Description* (1736), iii. 22.
‡ *Qanoon-e-Islam*, 254.

For the purpose of ascertaining where stolen goods are concealed, or the condition of the sick who are possessed by the devil, or where treasure has been buried, they apply unjun to the palms of the hand of a child or an adult, and desire him to stare well at it. This is practised, it is said, by Yogis and Sunnecasses.

" Unjuns are of five kinds—viz. (1) *Urth unjun*, used for discovering stolen property; (2) *Bhoot unjun*, for ascertaining what regards evil spirits, devils, and the condition of the sick ; (3) *Duhuna unjun*, for finding out where treasure is concealed ; (4) *Sinwa unjun*, for all purposes ; (5) *Alope unjun*, which is applied to the eyes or forehead of a person, renders him invisible to others while they remain visible to him."

For 1 and 2 take the root of *achyranthes aspera* Linn. and white *abrus precatorius*, or else of *trianthema decandra* Willd. Triturate it well with water, rub it on the inside of a new earthen pot, and place it inverted over a lamp lighted with castor oil, and collect the lamp-black. The latter is then mixed with oil, and applied to the hand of a footling child, who can then describe what is required.

For 3 a piece of white cloth soaked in the blood of a cat, a king-crow, or an owl was required. In it were to be rolled their eyes, liver, and gall bladder, and the whole was to be used as the wick of a castor-oil lamp, and the lamp-black used as

D

before. For 4 a handful of seed of *dolichos lablab* tar is required, which must be reduced to charcoal in a new earthen pot, and well mixed with castor oil. After three quarters of an hour or so he will say : "First, I observe the *furash* (sweeper) coming; he swept the ground, and departed. Then came the water-carrier ; he sprinkled water on the floor, and departed. Then the *furash* reappeared, and spread the carpet. Next came a whole array of fairies, genii, demons, etc. ; and then their commander seated on a throne." To this commander must be put the question or questions to which answers are needed.

Anyone can try this method. For the others a child born foot foremost, with cats' (*i.e.* grey, according to the work quoted) eyes, and a first-born who has not been bitten by a dog and has no large scar of a burn upon him.

Another way of divining is by the viewing of *hazirat* or the charm-wick. For this method certain charm-wicks, called *puleeta*, must be used. A new earthen pot must be taken, and an earthen cover, well washed, with a few patches of sandalwood embrocation. Wreaths of flowers must be tied round its neck and all sorts of fruit and sweetmeats put near it, and, further, pastilles must be burnt near it. The cover may then be put on the pot, and some sweet oil into the lid ; then light the *puleeta*, and read some established spell over it in Arabic.

The boy or girl must bathe, and be decked out in clean clothes and adorned with flowers. He or she then stares at the flame.

Some people use a spell pasted on the back of a looking-glass, into which the child looks. The following is recommended :—

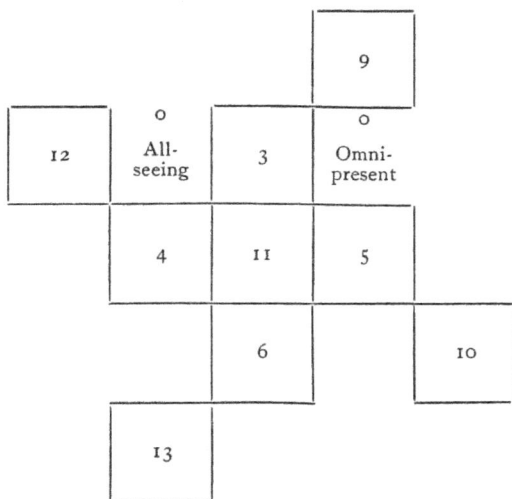

		9	
12	o All-seeing	3	o Omni-present
	4	11	5
		6		10
	13		

Others write a magic square on a porcelain or copper plate, fill it with water, and desire the child to look into it. Such a magic square is :

4	9	2
3	5	7
8	1	6

Some people, while performing any of these ceremonies, write on the child's forehead: " We have removed the veil from thee, and thy sight is become new this day. Come, genius, Jaffier, son of Tyar." Another incantation is : " In the name of God, merciful and compassionate, Ushteetun, Shuteetun, Kubooshin, Shaleesha, Sheeshin, Qoorbutashin, Murmoonin, Mymoonin."

According to a statement by Colonel A. T. Fraser, the whole of the Hindu methods are termed Unjamu. One way of inducing the visions is to put a spot of a pitchy substance, made up with castor oil, on a green leaf, and stick it against the wall.*

In Africa crystal gazing seems to be common. Mr Lang cites a case from Madagascar where a woman is alleged to have seen a French vessel on its way thither, and to have recognised its occupants, weeks before the ship was in sight of land. The Africans of Fez used a vessel of water, and we shall see that at the present day a pool of ink is in use in Egypt. The most singular account of crystal or rather mirror gazing comes from the Nkomis of the neighbourhood of Cap Lopez, who are remarkable for practising a species of blood bond between a man and an animal, if my authority can be trusted.†

In this tribe the initiant, as a rule, goes far away from his village for the ceremony, and, like all savage

* *Jl. S.P.R.* iv. 149.
† Buléon, *Sous le ciel d'Afrique,* 88 et seq.

youth undergoing the ceremony, he has to undergo a fast as one of the essential features. A fast,
it may be noted, is one of the important points in
the initiation ceremony of the Red Indians, and in
their case the end of it is that some bird or beast
(hallucinatory) appears to the boy, and this becomes
his " medicine," or tutelary deity. In many cases
he has to kill it, and carry about in his medicine bag
a claw, a feather, or some part of it, which he must
never lose, on pain of losing his medicine.

Among the Nkomis the ordeal is more severe.
The initiant is confined in a hut, at one end of which
is a rude image of wood. Beneath the statue is
deposited a packet containing the bones of someone
long dead, and in front a looking-glass. The initiant
is brought up to this mirror, and asked to describe
what he sees, and as long as he replies " Nothing "
his initiation is incomplete. When he answers
that he sees the face of a man he is taken aside, and
asked to describe him, and if he succeeds in describing
the dead man whose bones are in the bundle he is
at liberty to proceed to the next step—the meeting
with an animal in the forest, and the transfusion of
blood, which is necessary to seal the blood bond.
Sometimes, however, a ceremony intervenes between
the scrying and the blood bond which recalls the
Red Indian custom. The initiator calls upon the
initiant to bring the skull or some of the bones of
one of his relatives, the flesh of which is then cooked

and consumed, while the initiant receives the bones as a talisman. According to the author whom I quote, and whose death, unfortunately, prevented me from ascertaining further details, there is no possibility of fraud in the scrying part of the ceremony. The initiant has never seen the person whose bones lie beneath the statue, and yet his description is unmistakable. One may suspect, however, that a hint may be purchased from the initiator, just as steps in the secret societies, of which the ceremonies described are, perhaps, part of the ritual, are habitually purchased in Africa, Melanesia, and other parts of the world.

If we could rely on the good faith of the initiator the case would, of course, be of much interest. There are narratives, some of which I have at first hand from persons immediately concerned with the proceedings, of ghosts having been laid by the simple process of burying their bones, the presence of which, immured in some old convent wall or other inaccessible and invisible hiding-place, could only be inferred from the presence of the ghost. Perhaps suggestion may explain the result. In other cases the removal of a skeleton from a house has likewise resulted in laying the ghost, though in this latter case we may discount the result, which may also be attributed to suggestion. Of course, the suggestion theory fails in the first case to explain the presence of the ghost, and in the second case has to call in the help of a secondary theory of physical effluvium from the bones to explain why the inmates should have suffered from hauntings.

In the case before us the Nkomi believe, in theory at any rate, that the bringing of the bones of a dead man will result in bringing his ghost; or, if not his ghost, at any rate his veridical apparition in the mirror.

Consequently, it is very unfortunate that the facts cannot be better established. Père Buléon's successor is a Gallio, and cares neither for anthropology nor psychical research.

We have already seen from Ibn Kaldoun that the liver was gazed at to provoke hallucinations. Mr Lang found the same method in Assam.

Among the Berbers at the time of the Greek Empire was a mirror, which was kept in a church; it was said to have the property of showing a man who mistrusted his wife upon whom he should keep an eye. After the Berbers had embraced Christianity one of them, distinguished by his zeal, was made a deacon. A Berber who consulted the mirror saw in it the said deacon's face, and lost no time in citing him before the Emperor, who condemned the deacon, in accordance with the gentle manners of the times, to have his nose cut off, and to be marched in procession. His compatriots, irritated at his degradation, broke the mirror;

whereupon the Emperor marched troops against them, and exterminated them.*

On the Gold Coast at the present day the magician looks for the cause of a disease in a vessel of water.†

On the Congo, when Maloango dies, the Mamboma of Loango calls together all the other Mambomas to elect a king in the stead of the dead Maloango. If they come to an agreement, well and good. If not, they go to the sacred grove of Mpuku Nyambi, the nephew of Bunzi (a mythological character), and there consult his *nganga* or priest, whose head-dress is made of parrot feathers and small mirrors.

The *nganga*, on being consulted, removes his head-dress, gazes into a mirror, and sees in it the face of the Maloango elect. In Europe there might be some suspicion of backstairs influence if such a method were adopted. Is the negro more credulous, or more honest ?

When there is a drought upon the land the King of Congo goes to the same sacred grove to ask the reason. The *nganga* looks at his mirror, and is then able to say if it is " god palaver " (*i.e.* due to the caprice of their god), or if man has occasioned it by his misdeeds.‡

Another Arab author says that in a mirror angels and archangels will appear, from whom one can

---

* *Notices des MSS.* xii. 484.
† *Mag. für die neueste Geschichte,* 1856, 138.
‡ MS. note from R. E. Dennett.

obtain all that one desires.   On the side of the mirror must be written the names Gabriel, Michael, Azrael, Asrafel, with some words of the Koran which, being translated, mean " His word is true and his is the power." Incense must be burnt, and a fast of seven days undergone, and then someone must hold the mirror, or one may hold it oneself. After the recitation of certain prayers the angel will appear.*

A Persian novel, called " The Springtime of Knowledge," mentions a mirror which was covered with ink when anyone desired to see anything.

Various Persian authors relate, quite seriously, that Gemschid and his successors possessed a cup, or rather a globe or mirror, in which could be seen the whole universe.†

According to Mustadha, the Pharaohs had a similar instrument, in which they discovered the state of distant provinces, and were able to provide against famines.   It was said to have been made by the order of Saurid, the son of Sahaloc, and was set " in a high turret of brass in the midst of ancient Masre, which is Emsos."‡

Alexander is said to have put a mirror on the lighthouse of Alexandria in which objects could be perceived even at a distance of several days' journey :

* *MSS. Arabes de la Bibl. du roi,* 1203, fol. 226.
† Bonomi, p. 266 ; see also *Vera Historia,* i. 26.
‡ Mustadha ibn al Khafif, *Egyptian History,* p. 26.

Aristotle was said to have made it. On the subject of this mirror Norden says that Arab authors stated its circumference to be 3 ft. 9 in. ; some said it was of crystal, others of polished Chinese steel or an alloy of different metals.*

In the same way the Colossus of Rhodes was said to have a mirror round its neck by which they could see ships on their way to Syria and Egypt.†
Hercules was said to have founded Corunna and placed there a tower and a mirror by which the most distant ships could be seen.‡

In Mexico the god Tezcatlipoca was believed to see in his golden mirror, *itlachia* (the looker-on or viewer), all the doings of the world.§

In Europe Merlin's mirror showed friends and foes, whether near or far ; and Cambuscan's showed whether love were returned, what trouble was in store for the scryer, and whether a person were friend or foe. In the Gesta Romanorum is the story of a knight who went to Palestine, and was shown by an Eastern magician what was going on at home.

Joseph's divining cup, too, must be mentioned, though it by no means follows that he used it for crystal gazing. The appearance of the liquid, or

* Norden, *Voyage d'Egypte*, Paris, 1795, iii. 163 ; Jean Leon, *Desc. de l'Afrique*, Anvers, 1556, fol. 358.
† Bouchet, G. *Série* xix. pp. 171, 172.
‡ L. Nonnius, *Hispania*, p. 196.
§ Bancroft, iii. 238.

of oil floating on it, was used for divination, or pieces of gold and silver thrown in.*

Of the magic " mirror on the wall," which tells " who is the fairest of them all," we most of us have heard in our childhood.

NOTE TO CHAPTER V

In that store of ancient folklore maxims known as the Symbols of Pythagoras, the interpreting and perverting of which taxed the ingenuity of many generations of scholiasts and classical scholars, we find a recommendation not to look at one's face in the river nor to wash it therein. The wisdom of the commentator has discovered in this an allusion to the mutability and impermanency of the things of this world, and the modern rationalist might be inclined to say that the precept was a wise one, for the incautious might tumble in.

But in all probability the explanation lies in the facts of crystal gazing or hypnotism. We find the same injunction in the laws of Manu; and the Greek fable of Narcissus, who pined away for love of his own image reflected in the water is probably an etherealised form of the same belief. In " The Golden Bough " (i. 285 *et seq*.) Dr Frazer has abundantly illustrated the savage belief that a person's shadow or reflection is his soul; and if my

* *See* Bouché Leclercq, *Histoire* ; Lenormant, *La Magie*.

suggestion is right this view, like so many other savage theories, rests on a misinterpreted groundwork of fact.

More explicit on the question of gazing into water is the Bavarian belief,* which asserts that if one lies in the grave for three hours, or if a child gazes long into a glass of water " die Bermǝte † kōmt aus dem Häus'l," the soul quits its abode.

The emphasis here laid on the fact that a child is more subject to the disaster makes it clear that the foundation of the belief in crystal gazing is hypnotism; for it is a well-known fact that children are more readily hypnotised than adults, and, as mediæval records show, the superiority of the juvenile scryer has long been recognised.

A cognate subject is the practice of covering up mirrors after a death. Some of Dr Frazer's examples are explicit in assigning as the cause his fear that the soul of the living, projected into the glass, may be carried off by the dead. But it is by no means improbable that in part the belief rests on the facts of crystal gazing.

In the census of hallucinations the examples are fairly numerous in which the apparition, coincidental or otherwise, has been seen in a mirror or other bright object. When we consider that for

* Panzer, *Beitrag*, ii. 195. In the New Hebrides they say that if you look into water a snake will come and seize your tongue. (*R. Geog. Soc. Vict.* x. 54).

† =Gebärmutter, properly uterus, but here soul.

the Eskimo, the Red Indian, and others the apparition of a spirit is equivalent to giving the seer power
over that spirit, another explanation of the practice
of covering up mirrors suggests itself. The Indian
youth at initiation is able, by the magic power of
his fast, to summon the spirit of the animal which
is afterwards his " medicine." The savage all the
world over avoids mentioning the name of the dead,
for by the magic power of the name, which some
savages carefully conceal, the dead man may be
summoned. Every well-brought-up child knows
that to mention a bogie is to run a great risk of
bringing the bogie to the spot; and the Papuans
hold the same view, as a story in the Report of
the Cambridge Anthropological Expedition shows,
where a party of New Guinea youths and maidens,
after playing hockey, Ladies *v.* Gentlemen, on the
beach, return home, and one luckless maid, finding
that her mother has cooked the second-best fish for
her admirer, who goes back with her to tea, sits
down and weeps, and will not be comforted. In
an ill-advised moment someone mentions a bogie,
apropos of a heartless practical joke of the village
lads, who are imitating outside the traditional
bogie noises, and in less than no time the bogie is on
the spot, and carries off the tearful maiden.

Thus the fear of summoning spirits and monsters,
and the belief in the possibility of compelling them,
is a very common one. All the world over man

has discovered that he can see visions in a clear, deep, or bright object. It seems possible that the practice of covering up a mirror was due to the fear of summoning the dead, though the dread of losing the souls of the living may have contributed its quotum to making the custom popular.

CHAPTER VI

Crystal gazing among the Greeks and Romans—
Mediæval and modern scrying—Gastromancy—
Onymancy—Scrying and statecraft—The Faust
books—Bergspiegel—Other methods

ALTHOUGH we have but few notices of crystal gazing
among the Greeks and Romans. it would be rash
to infer from this that the practice was uncommon
among them. But for the Symbols of Pythagoras
we should know very little of the popular super-
stitions of the ancients; yet these precepts, to which
we shall return later, are nothing but a collection
of the wisdom of the folk, and would be readily
intelligible to the present-day savage—far more
readily, in fact, than to the commentators who
have surpassed themselves in discovering allegorical
meanings for the simplest savage ideas, such as that
you should not look into deep water.

Pausanias tells us of a practice at the temple of
Demeter at Patræ on the coast of Achaia. Before
the temple was a fountain famous for the accuracy
of its oracles. It was consulted mainly for the
sick, and not indiscriminately, so there is some

doubt as to whether we have to do with crystal or mirror gazing, or rather with some other form of divination. The manner of divining was this : A mirror was lowered into the fountain by a small cord until the lower edge just touched the water but was not covered by it. Prayers and incense were then offered to the goddess, and recourse was had to the mirror, from whose reflections and images they drew conclusions as to the patient's chances.*

According to Augustine, Varro says that Numa practised hydromancy, and saw in the water the images of the gods or rather sports of demons, from which he learnt what rites to perform. Unless an older authority is quoted this evidence is, of course, as valueless as the remark of a later commentator that the myth of Numa's marriage with Egeria clearly referred to this practice, for she was a nymph of the fountains, and consequently a fit mate for one who divined by means of water.†

Diogenes tells us in the life of Isidorus that a woman had a marvellous gift of inspiration, for by filling a vessel with water she was able to see all future things, and prophesied from her vision what should come to pass, and the truth of these prophecies was known to the writer himself.

In another story related by Varro we hear of a

* *Pausanias*, VII. xxi. 12.
† *De Civ. Dei.*

child who was consulted as to the war with Mithridates.* Spartianus tells of a prophecy given by a child, whose eyes were bandaged, and who was, nevertheless, able to scry in a mirror by means of the top of his head, just as some of the early hypnotists record cases of transferred sensation. The only thing that one does not understand is why it was necessary to have a mirror if the picture were hallucinatory.†

Andronicus Comnenus had recourse to a hydromantic diviner to discover his successor, whom he intended to dispose of by violent means at the first opportunity. The water, as is sometimes the case with the crystal in the hands of present-day scryers, gave such messages as were vouchsafed mirrorwise—in other words, the letters S I, which formed the whole of the first answer, and were interpreted to mean Isaac Angelus, appeared in reverse order. The prediction was verified; but perhaps the scryer had a shrewd suspicion as to the probable course

* Apuleius, *Apol*, 41.

† Spartian. *Did. Jul.* vii. At Segarme, in Brie, a poor labourer, from whom had been stolen six hundred francs, consulted a diviner, whose fee was twelve francs. Three handkerchiefs were put on his eyes—black, white, and blue—and the diviner told him to describe what he saw. The peasant described a man with a blue blouse, broad-brimmed hat, and grey trousers, and was directed to take an ox's heart and stick sixty nails in it, and boil it in a new pot with a toad and a leaf of sorrel. Three days later the thief should have been dead, or bewitched, or have brought back the money.—*Plancy* i. 237.

E

of events, for Comnenus was by no means popular.*

Apropos of the story from Spartianus narrated above, Casaubon tells a story of a Latin Christian who was mortified by the too frequent success of the opposite faction in the games. With the aid of Hilarion, a monk of exceptional piety, he discovered that the horses and chariots, which he saw in the water, were under a spell. Hilarion having dissipated this with the sign of the cross, his client went on his way rejoicing ; but whether the remedy was successful we do not know.†

About 450 A.D. we find that a synod convened by St Patrick and St Auxentius condemned Christians who believed there was a " lamia " or witch in the mirror.‡ In the ninth century Hincman speaks of hydromancy in which images of demons are seen and their replies heard. § Three hundred years later John of Salisbury tells us that those who looked in cups or basons, or at mirrors or bright swords, were called specularii ; and he gives a list of procedures against them.||

About the same time Thomas Aquinas assures us that the peculiar gift of seeing visions, to which there are many allusions, was not a result of their

* Nicetas, *A.C.* ii. 19.
† *Casaubon Spartianum*, vii. 250.
‡ Ducange, *s.v. Specularii.*
§ *De Divortio Hlotarii* in *Migne*, 125, 718.
|| John of Salisbury, *Polyc.* I. xii.

innocence but of the machinations of the devil, who desired in this way to get them into his power.

The Inquisition busied itself with the question of whether Christians were guilty of heresy if they caused boys or girls to scry in glass vessels, or with lighted candles in their hands to look into water in order to discover a thief, or to put oil on their hands, and scry in this way ; the accepted view seems to have been that such persons were guilty of heresy. In fact, it is distinctly laid down that even if both the candle and the water be consecrated, and the scryer repeat " Angelo bianco, Angelo santo, per la tua santita, per la mia virginita," the offence is not the less heretical.*

In the *Buch aller verbotenen Kunst*, published in 1465, we find scrying mentioned under the name of pyromancy, though there seems to have been nothing fiery employed, the only specula mentioned being mirrors, brightly-polished swords, crystals and beryls, which are said to be consecrated before use and censed.

In the following century the *Neupolierte Geschichtkunst* says : " It is known that in many towns old women, and men, too, at times, show to people, on whom God's wrath should fall, in mirrors and crystals what they desire to see. Thus at Elbingen, in Prussia, there was one a few years ago. These old sibyls are on confidential terms with Black

* Egerton MSS. 1090, fol. 5 ; *cf.* Görres, *Mystik*, iii.

Caspar, and with the help of this evil spirit can show the issue of future events."

Girolamo Cardano (1501-1573) mentions that he tried an experiment with his son, John the Baptist, then nine years of age : smearing his palm with oil and soot, or lamp-black, he exposed it to the rays of the sun, and on being asked the boy asserted that he saw visions, as, indeed, he did, in all probability ; the father, however, saw nothing, and remained a doubting Thomas. A few pages later he mentions capnomancy, a species of divination usually unconnected with crystal visions, but understood by our author to mean the discerning of figures and images in the smoke by virgins and matrons.*

Girolamo Cardano describes elsewhere † some other experiments which he witnessed. A bottle filled with holy water was placed on a table covered with a white cloth, in the sun ; two olive leaves were crossed over its mouth, and three wax candles were lighted. During certain fumigations a prayer to St Helena was offered, and soon the adepts saw forms in the water—a bald-headed man, and a man dressed in scarlet. Cardano himself saw nothing.

* *De Sapientia* 268, 271.

It may be mentioned that Cardano and Peucer speak of so-called " physical phenomena " in connection with water gazing. If the " gastromant " covers his head with a white cloth and says certain spells the water will boil up and disappear.

† *De Var.*

Peucer speaks of lecanomancie—divination by basins.* Gold and silver plate and precious stones, marked with certain characters, were put in, and a spirit called and questioned. It made itself heard by a thin voice : " Comme un sifflet sortant de l'eau, laquelle respondoit à la demande."

Of gastromancy he says : " En ceste-ci (qu'on pourroit exposer diuination par le fond, asauoir d'un verre ou autre chose transparente, le mot de ventre se prenant ici par figure pour chose creuse), le malin esprit respondit par peintures et repré-sentations. On disposoit des vaisseaux de verre, faits en forme ronde et remplis d'eau clère, alentour desquels estoyent bien des cierges allumez. Puis, ayant inuoqué l'esprit par un secret barbottement, l'on auoit un petit garçon vierge ou un femme enceinte qui considéroit le verre attentivement, regardant tout autour, prioit, commandoit, et faisoit instance pour avoir response, lesquelles en-fin le diable donnoit par des images empraintes dedans l'eau, qui se monstroyent par l'artifice du diable, au travers les verres clairs et luisants. Ceste façon de deuiner a l'aide des enfants vierges, qui a esté fort usitée anciennement et est encores aui-ourdhui pratiquée entre des peuples profanes, a esté desirée et requise par l'esprit immonde et malin, non qu'il aime la chasteté, ains pour preparer et dis-poser d'heure à son service et polluer ainsi de leur

* Peucer, *Les Devins* (1553), p. 221.

bas aage les âmes chastes et innocentes, brief pour attirer et enueloper en ses filez ceux qui a cause de leur simplesse ne se peuuent garder de luy."

Of divination by the finger nails he says : " Ony-mance se faisoit avec de l'huile et de la suye, dont on frottoit l'ongle d'un petit garçon vierge, que l'on faisoit tourner vers le soleil. Car ils pensoyent que les figures des choses desirées se fissent par le mes-lange de l'huile, de la suye et des rayons du soleil, encores qu'elles fussent faites par l'imposture du diable."

An anonymous German work, called the 138 *Kunststücke*, written in the seventeenth century, says: " Zu der zeit eines glorwürdigsten damals regie-renden Monarchen [Kaiser Rudolph II., 1552-1612], came an Italian to his chamberlain, and offered through him a secret to the emperor, by which he could tell what the king of France did in his most secret cabinet." The emperor was not to be per-suaded, but is said to have given the Italian 1000 Reichsthalers, and sent him away. The chamber-lain, on the other hand, was less conscientious, and secured the secret, which consisted in making a young boy or a virgin conjure St Cyprian to let them see Solomon in their hands ; and there Solomon ap-peared in their hands, with his red beard, on his throne, with his sceptre in one hand, and a dagger in the other, a minister on either side. When this apparition had made its appearance the scryer put his hand over his ear, and then asked his question, and Solomon answered.

An early mediæval case of crystal gazing is that recorded by Spengler, according to whom a noble Nürnberger brought him a crystal wrapped in a cloth, saying that a stranger had given it to him many years before in gratitude for his hospitality. He had, so he said, made many trials of the power of his glass to disclose the whereabouts of lost articles, and never failed of success, his scryer being a boy, and on one occasion his wife. The first thing that became visible was the form of a man, and he remained during the whole scry ; they often saw the person [in the crystal] going through the streets and into the churches, obviously in his search for the lost articles. The crystal was frequently appealed to when anyone concealed the truth or a crime, and on one occasion a party of savants read in the crystal the answer to a problem that had perplexed them.

The noble, after using the crystal for many years, seems to have been seized with scruples in his old age, and that was why he brought it to Spengler, who broke it in pieces, and disposed of it.

The chief source of our knowledge of Continental crystal gazing in the Middle Ages is the Faust literature.

Students of the Faust legend are aware that a great part of the literature attributed to him is apocryphal. Among the most authentic of his Faust books, however, is the authentic *Höllenzwang* (there are spurious editions of this too), a collection of magical recipes, which was certainly in print in the first years of the seventeenth century (the historical Faust lived in the first half of the sixteenth).

Four chapters of the *Höllenzwang* deal with crystal gazing and allied subjects—lxvii., lxx., lxxi., and lxii. The first of these is concerned with the famous Erdspiegel, or Bergspiegel, a mirror which was intended to show all the hidden treasures of the earth. The directions for the preparation of this are as follows :—Buy a new mirror on a Friday, and pay for it whatever the vendor asks, in order that no evil spirit may injure it ; bury it in a man's grave in a churchyard at midnight, exactly on the face of the dead man, and let it lie there nine Fridays. On the ninth go back, and take it out. Go to the cross-roads, and lay it in the middle, in the name of three spirits, choosing them according to the nature of the service required ; thus for treasures hid in the earth you must name Ariel and Marbuel, for they are swift messengers. After them name Aciel, who will show you the treasure, and keep off all attendant spirits ; and, what is more, show you how to get the treasure, how much there is of it, and what it consists of. Here, too, the mirror must remain for nine Fridays, and then the three spirits

PLATE III.]

1

2

3

must be put into it, care being taken that the operator does not see into it himself. The words of the spell are completely different from those of the spells used in England, as will be seen by the following quotation :—" I, N., ban thee, spirit Ariel, thee spirit Aciel, thou spirit Marbuel into my mirror in the name of Rore + ipse + Loisant + and Dortam + Bolaimy + Acom + Coelum + Quiavitil + Sammas + Restacia + o Adonay + o Jehova + prasa Deus. I conjure you by Rolamicon + Hipite + Agla + Elohim + Reremisch . . . by Scham Schmachadaz + Maaschmay + Ischalam + Ischaylam . . . by Adonay Agla + Paaschilam + o Aglam + Ischailas + Cassrielis + o Jehovah + Schailis + o Amisielis + o Sadalachia + o Arielis + o Cassrielis + o Gabrielis + amenisch."

Then the mirror must lie three Sundays on the altar, but beware of allowing a blessing of the dead to be said over it. Finally, engrave under the mirror the characters shown on Plate III., and it is ready for use.

For a mirror to be used for divination take a round piece of iron like a mirror, and have it polished ; then get a similar piece, unpolished, to lay on the first mirror, so that you can't see into it. On the top of them lay a piece of wood or paper, and cense them, and let a priest read the gospel of John over them. Then cut the wood or the paper so as to fit the mirror into it, and write Tetragrammaton and various other words thereon. Various names must then be said, and the mirror is ready.

In the seventy-second chapter directions for crystal gazing are given. The crystal must be crossed with olive oil, and a prayer said to St Helena—this at sunrise. A boy of ten or eleven must take the crystal in his right hand, and he will be able to see what you desire.

Another method (useful for discovering a thief) is to take a glass bowl, or rather vase, and fill it with holy water, put it on a bench covered with consecrated cloth, and light three wax candles. On the mouth of the vase lay crosswise two olive leaves, and say the Paternoster on your knees. Then make a cross with the right thumb nail on the mouth of the vase, all in the dark, and say a prayer.

The seventy-first chapter gives still another method, which must be tried in a solitary place, where no cockcrow nor sound of church bell can be heard. On a Friday, by waxing moon, put on clean clothes, take a clean glass, and fill it with water. Cover it with a linen cloth, and set it on a marble slab, and say a prayer or spell over it, calling upon a spirit to enter it. As soon as he is in, close the glass hermetically with wax, and keep him there. In this spell the magic names are again different— Zoyma, Zoplay, Pastorem, Coronem, Primonem; and if the spell is not effectual go on for a whole hour, and finally a beautiful man or woman will appear. He will fetch what you want, even human beings, and will take you over land and sea, and bring you back unharmed in body and soul.

Finally, chapter seventy-two gives directions for the preparation of a crystal of metal or glass, which is, however, not so powerful as a mirror. For the use of this Mephistopheles himself must be present, he says, and Azeruel and Adadiel. They can show stolen things, give diagnoses of illnesses, disclose evil magic, and so on. The characters to be inscribed on the crystal are shown on Plate LIII., figure 2.

Another method is to buy a crystal, and lay it in holy water with which a first-born boy has been baptised; let it lie in it three weeks; pour the water away in a churchyard, and read John vi. over the glass, and then the following spell :—" Crystal, thou art pure as a young maiden, thou standest at the gate of heaven, and nothing is hid from thee, be it on field or meadow, be it master or servant, be it mistress or maid," etc.

The same seventy-second chapter gives an account of how to summon the nine aerial spirits, whose names are Nector, Goeme, Monto, Cassessi, Hassica, Mentanta, Husro, Fos, and Fahassur. A glass must be filled with spring water on any day but Saturday or Sunday, with the moon in Gemini, Libra, or Aquarius, and by good weather. The spirits' names are then to be written in gold, or some yellow fluid, or, better, with the blood of a black hen or a black lamb, on new parchment. If the scryer and the director of the operation can sing or play, so much the better. Face the east, sprinkle hands and face with rose water, and call upon the spirits. The first eight will appear, and they will fetch their king, to whom you must say : " Herr König, Ew. Königl. Majestät wollen wir mit gott willkommen seyn, sammt den lieben angehörigen dienern." The king is then asked to fetch the throne and book of Solomon, and take a solemn oath to answer truly ; if he did so he was not to be kept beyond the proper time.

He will then answer you with legible writing, or show you the person you desire. When you have got your information you inquire of the king if he wishes to partake of refreshment, and if the answer is in the affirmative ask him to send the servants to fetch food and drink from the kitchen of A. B. The meal ended, the king is thanked and dismissed, the water poured away in a clean place, and the vessel put away till it is next required.

The account goes on that the apparition may be cited to appear in a crystal, a mirror, or in the hand. In the latter case oil and soot should be taken and smeared upon the hand. Then go to a dark place with a wax candle, and you will then see the figures. If the scryer is a boy, the names of the spirits—Gardiab, Fardiar, and Ipodhar—must be said in his ear three times, and also written on parchment, and tied round his arm.

There are innumerable other references to crystal gazing in Continental authors, some of whom, such as Rist, tell interesting stories, unfortunately non-evidential, of prophecies told by means of a crystal, with a love interest running through the story. We read of Jacob Böhme that he scryed " in the lovely, jovial lustre of the cup," and was enabled to look into the hearts of all creatures.

As a rule, however, we find nothing but wearisome repetition, nearly the self-same words of what has been said by fifty predecessors.

Aubrey gives one or two cases which show that crystal gazing flourished in Italy.*

When Sir Marmaduke Langdale was in Italy he went to one of these Magi, who did show him a glass where he saw himself kneeling before a crucifix. He was then a Protestant, and afterwards became a Roman Catholic.

The Earl of Denbigh, then Ambassador at Venice, did tell James Harrington that one did show him several things in a glass—things past and to come.

As a rule, however, there is little that is worth quoting, and we may pass to the subject of scrying in England during the Middle Ages.

There cannot be much doubt that crystal gazing was as well known in England in the Middle Ages

* Aubrey, p. 219.

as it was on the Continent. English authors, however, seem to have had better occupations than writing of divination and suchlike " works of the devil " ; consequently we do not find, until comparatively late, any literary references to the subject. In the next chapter will be quoted a MS. in the British Museum in a handwriting which fixes its date as some time early in the fifteenth century ; but it is not until the following century that references to it are frequent. From the time of Dr Dee (1527-1608) onward there is no lack of material for those who are fond of diving into old MSS. and works on magic. We have, however, dealt with Continental crystal gazing at such length that it will be unnecessary to say much of English scrying.

In the reign of Henry VIII. the Abbot of Abingdon wrote to Cromwell : " Right honorable & my very singuler good Maister, in my mooste humble wyse I comende me unto you. It shall please your maistership to be advertised that my Officers have taken here a Preyste, a suspect parson ; & with hym certeyn bokes of conjuracions, in the which ys conteyned many conclusions of that worke ; as fynding out of tresure hydde, consecrating of ryngs with stones in theym, & consecrating of a chrystall stone wherein a chylde shall lokke & see many thynges." *

But those who wish to study in detail the ideas

* Ellis, *Original Letters*, 3rd. S. iii. 41.

of this period on the subject of crystal gazing will do well to turn their attention to a large but entertaining volume by Meric Casaubon, who edited Dr Dee's diary, and provided us with a valuable book of reference. Those who cannot obtain the original volume will find some extracts from it in the paper by Miss Goodrich-Freer in the *Proc. S.P.R.* xiv. 494 *et seq.*

Glanvil in his "Saducismus" gives us some facts with regard to the crystal visions of a Mr Compton of Somersetshire, who asserts that a patient of his (he was a physician of some repute) had a veridical vision of his (Compton's) wife, with whom he was quite unacquainted.*

Other facts will be found in the " Life of Lilly," p. 234; Aubrey's " Miscellanies," p. 196; Scot's " Discovery of Witchcraft," and other works.

Coming down to the last century, we find that crystal gazing excited a good deal of interest in the fifties. Lady Blessington had a crystal, which the proprietor of Zadkiel's Almanac utilised, and his scryer professed, among other things, to see the position of Sir John Franklin's expedition. I have never had the curiosity to examine how far Zadkiel, who sued a British admiral for libel apropos of the latter's remarks on his crystal visions (v. *Times*, 30th June 1863), was right in his assertions. From the other facts in the Almanac of 1851 I am inclined

---

* *Saducismus Triumphatus*, pp. 202, 204.

to think not much reliance could be placed on him. Among other visions there appeared Sir Isaac Newton, to tell us that electricity was partly the cause of the moon's motion; various spirits who said they were in the abode of the just—Jupiter and the sun—of whom Calvin had been in Jupiter only a few weeks, and George IV. (verily Fortune makes us acquainted with strange bedfellows), for an unspecified period. Pharaoh and Harold were there too; while George III. and Zoroaster were in the sun. For some reason Washington and Captain Cook had taken refuge in the moon; but they were happy too. Judas and Alexander the Great were in a state of punishment; but they were the only unhappy ones, unless we except Socrates, who was compelled to appear in coarse, striped peg-top trousers. After this it naturally makes very little impression to hear that Orion came with a bear. His portrait is given, but I am bound to say he resembles the portraits of some of the Plantagenets in " A Child's History of England " rather than a Greek demi-god.

Even in those days visits to crystal gazers were fashionable; but from a writer in an early volume of *Household Words* we learn that titled ladies, fearing to disclose their identity, disguised themselves as charwomen to visit the scryers of the New Cut. When Bond Street became the resort of these modern magicians I cannot say.

Among curious cases of scrying the following case is probably unique:—A certain Dove, who was executed for the murder of his wife, possessed an egg-shaped crystal, which afterwards passed into the possession of H. Harrison of Leeds. Into this crystal the aforesaid Dove (by name though not by nature) gazed immediately before giving strychnine to his wife, but with what result history does not say.

F

CHAPTER VII

THE INCANTATION OR "CALL"

*Animistic theory—The power of the name—Priestly
help—Magic—To discover thieves or lost friends
—To compel runaways to return—Astrological
magic—*Raison d'être *of the "call"*

IN accordance with the animistic philosophy of
classical and mediæval times (which is shared by
some modern crystal gazers) the scryer's visions
are naturally held to be the work of spirits, or in
many cases to be the spirits themselves disporting
themselves before his eyes. This being so, it was
natural to ensure their presence by an incantation,
subsequently known as a " call," and to provide by
magical or other means against injury to man or
beast at the arrival and departure of the spirit.

We have no examples of classical crystal ritual
so far as I know. The earliest " call " I can
quote in English is from a MS. of the late fifteenth
century, but, of course, not necessarily composed
at that date. It runs as follows :—*

To yᵉ fydyng of theft or of the statt of fryndes or of tresure
hyddyn or not hyddyn or of other thyngs whatsoever they be

_____

* Sloane, 3849.

in yᵉ word yʷ shallte fyrst a chylde lawfullye borne wᵗ xii
years of age & a greatte crystall stone or byrrall holl & sond and
lett yt be anoyntyd wᵗ oylle olyve holowyd and than the chylde
shall say after the mʳ iii tyms Andromalce come thow wᵗ hast
& yᵗ   I may pceve yᵉ wᵗ my syght & other thyngs
    than say bn̄dicite Dn̄s. In noie prīs & fil (etc.)
    but fyrst cōsecrat yᵉ oylle thys maner.
I cōiure yᵉ oylle be yᵉ holye baptyme of god & be same holye
oyntment yᵗ iii maryes dyd beare to ye sepulcker yᵗ yᵉy myght
anoynt ye bodye of cryst burryed In lyke man̄ be yᵉ holdȳg
receyvyng suche vʳtue yᵗ spūs entrans into yⁱˢ stone yᵉ wch
compasse shall be anoyntyd yᵉy shal not have powʳ to hydde
the treweth but of shewyng openlye of all thyngs I shall
aske hym or yᵉᵐ to be Inquyryd of.—In nōīe prīs etc.   I
coniure yʳ Andromalcū be our lord yʳ father omnipotent, be yʳ
trewe god, be ye holye god, be god yᵉ wch. dyd cast yᵉ from
yᵉ joys of paradysse and be the name of god messias, Emanuell
otheos Athanatos ely panton craton & ysus alpha & ω Ihs
nazarenus χp̄s on el & be all yᵉ names of cryst & of god
/ I do coniure the Andromalcū be tetʳgramaton horoiall heon-
raldall abhoalsaual agla lamagaba thani Engoni legon gramaton
spirē Emirson And be holye Marye yᵉ mother of ouʳ lord Jhū
cryst & be yᵉ v Jois of here & be yᵉ vʳginitye of John the
evangelyst & be this name mapoth / napoth be ye wch Salamon
dyd close yow in a vessel of glass yᵗ whersoevʳ yʷ shalt be
nowe by & bye yʷ do entre into yⁱˢ cristal stone or glasse (yⁱˢ
glasse or stone) to ye syght of thys chylde in fayre forme of
mākynd havyng colour rede or whyte wᵗout any fear or hurt
of me or yᵉ chylde or any other beyng in yⁱˢ cōpany & wᵗout
grevans of body and solle. Amen. And yᵉⁿ ye mʳ shall sey
devoutly ye psalme. Deus in noie tuo resp. And yᵉⁿ ask ye
chylde yf hᵉ seethe any thyng / & yf no / let yᵉ mʳ begynne his
cōiuratyō agayn tyll he do come to ye second I cōiure yᵉ / yᵉⁿ
let yᵉ chyld say aftᵉʳ yᵉ mʳ iii tyms Andromalce come etc. yⁱˢ
done yᵉ mʳ shall say on / I cōmande yᵉ be yᵉ faythe yᵗ yʷ owyst
to yᵉ lord & ye private god be yᵉ v̄tue of yᵉ lyvyng god trewe &
puer & most m̄cifull & be yᵗ same Angyll yᵗ wh. dotħ syng
in a tube in yᵉ day of Judgementte & shall saye come yᵉ

blessyd. And be angylls & archangylls trons & ñatyons pñcipals pow^{rs} cherubyn & seraphyn & be all reliques of the sants and woomen sancts of god ye wch be cõteynyd in the world. And as mary was a trewe v̄gyne in here byrth and before & after & as y^t y^s trewe y^t ye host ye wch was brede ys cõvertyd into ye flesshe of our lord Jhu Xri & be the name ye wch be grettest in nigromãcia Balsake sup balsorke panulo in [ye pow^{er}] p^{rte} aye sarays serpasys to ye wch name watt^{er} be steyd & ye elementts be strykken & be thes name I cõmande y^e be the charytie of god, be ye eyes of hym & be all ye membres of hym & be ye deitye of hym & be ye good & evyll ye wch ye elyments doth suffre of them I do cõiure ye & yow y^t y^w shall std or ye shall sytt before me & y^{is} chylde in declarynge & shewyng to all ow^r [unde] answers & questons & in wryttyng y^t y^t wrytten may be to o^r understãdyng & full answers & satysfying to ow^r wyll and mynd And y^{en} as be what y^w wylt & y^w shalt have a answere & y^r secrete owght not to be shewed as y^w art wysse / And whan y^w shal be ãtysfyed of y^r mynd gyve to hym y^{is} lycense sayng I do cõiure ye Andrewemalce or you be all ye nams afore rehersyd that y^u dost go or you to ye place ye came from & whensoever I shall call you or any of you be ye redye Allways to me & come whan I call upon yow & ye peace of god but yt be betwen us & yow. In nõïe prïs etc.

> And let ye m^r say over ye chylde hede & he shall not be hurt nor any other beyng in his cõpanye & abowght hym sequencia s̄cti evangelii secūdū Johannem gtia tibi etc. inp^rncipio erat v̄bu & v̄bum erat ap^d deum.

A more approved method, however, was to address the spirits in Latin. A lengthy example, of which I quote only a portion, will be found in Sloane MS. 3848, f. 148, which is headed :

Here followeth an experyment approved & unknowne of Ascaryell to see most excellent and certainlye in a christall stoune what secrette thou wilt.

First take a christall stone or a glasse, the greater the better, so that it be fayre & cleare without any ragges, cracke or holes broken within it and thou must have a thonge of hart skinn to wrappe thy stoune in so that thy stoune may be well seene in the middst of the bindinge & ever before thou dost wrappe the stoune about with the thonge say thus : In nomine sanctae trinitatis et deitatis hanc gemam recondo. Then holde the christall stoune with it so dight in thy right hand against the O [*i.e.* the sun] wch. must be done in the heat of the O at noone when the O is in the highest & hottest and soe call him in such likeness as thou wilt by the conjuration followinge & he will come and show thee what thou wilt in all the countryes of all thinges whatsoever thou wilt ask him & thou shalt comannd him to bringe his followers with him and he will bring one Malhaperto with him and another also will come with them.

Sequitur conjuratio.

The conjuration begins : " Coniuro vos, centony, ceton, messitone, messiton, myssyron vel myceteron, qui habitatis in Bosco," and calls upon the spirits known by these remarkable names, and in particular upon a certain Askaryell, to appear in the crystal, on pain of being sent into the fire that is not quenched until the day of judgment.

After reeling off a list of biblical phrases, intended to influence the comings and goings of the said spirit, the operator proceeds to quote an amazing collection of names, supposed to be those of God. I give a selection of them, and offer a prize to the readers who can discover their original meaning: Ehel, Abiel, Anathael, Amay, hagyos, otheos, Deus, omnium potentias, hiecteta, gramaton, oneytheon, Almaron, Stimulaton, Elioram, Elsophares, existon historion, Rusus, Leabacon, Cryon, Elibra, Saton, Leccom, Leyste, Letisbon, Almarias, Rabur, Onela, Elbrac, Egepate, Abraca, Bota, Legeta Amazim, Saday, Elfel, Helenon, Abecor, ye, ya, El, Saray, Ymas, Anabona, and so on.

Not satisfied with this the operator proceeds to let loose a flood of so-called " secret names " of God, which are more suggestive of the Latin grammar than of anything else: Agnus, ovis, vitulus, aries, panis, flos, vitis, mons, pons, janua, petra, panton, kraton, igerion, albinago, talsea, and so on.

Should the conjuration not be successful the operator is advised to repeat the call three times. " And if he come not at the third call condempe him thus," and then follows a decree banishing the unfortunate Askaryell to the lake of unquenchable fire. On the supposition that a day or two of this will be enough to reduce him to obedience, it is suggested that the operator should call him a second day, and, if he come not, a third day, and so on until he come.

In another Sloane MS. (3851, f. 50 b) we find the assistance of the priest is to be invoked (the document is post-Reformation, but obviously a copy of an older prescription), and the crystal laid on the altar, " on the side that the gospell is read on. And let the priest say a mass on the same Side."

A few pages earlier * we find directions for trying whether the " angels " be true or false (Dr Dee was satisfied that they were true if they appeared in the crystal) ; if they are untrue they are to be cursed, and they will depart.

As a rule, the crystal visions of these old scryers seem to have been remarkably persistent. In the same MS. we read :

These angells being once appeared will not depart the glasse or stone untill the Sonne be sett except you licence them. Therefore if you call them at the sonne rising they will all that day be reddie to answer your demands untill the Sonne setting of the same day.

These gifted scryers were, however, few, for the MS. goes on :

If thou have the gift to have sight thyselfe it

* Sloane. 3851, f. 40.

is a Blessing that God giveth to very few. But to those that have it in their infancie and those often time lose it againe. But Prayer and a good beleefe prevaileth much. For faith is the cay to this and all other works, and without it nothinge can be effected.

The child should not be above 12 yeares of age, when you enter him or hir, for you may worke as well with a maid as with a boy.

When you have caled either angell or spirit, except you presently send them about some speedy busines you must licence them to depart.

In other words, the influence of suggestion was necessary to keep the crystal vision from vanishing.

In some of the conjurations we have clear survivals of older incantations, with no trace of the Christian influence which was so prominent in those just cited, or, as more often happens, there is an amalgam of magic and Christianity ; by trying the effect of both religion and magic they were, it is clear, doubling, on this theory, the chance of getting a spirit of some sort into the crystal. We have already seen a white hen figuring in the procedure of the Ashmolean MS. A Sloane MS. * directs you to take a black chicken if you wish.

To have a glasse wherein all menne may see theire desiers. Take a blacke chicken and put the

* 3850

same into a potte of erthe and then goe to a crosse waie and make theare an hole 3 foote deepe and put therin the pot with the chicke and then saie : crirma, crirma or crisma, crisma, I coniure the in the name of the Father and of the Sonne and of the Holie Ghoste and of his deathe & passion that died on the Tree, and by heaven and erthe & by the supernal pitte of Helle and by all that is therin contayned, that thou leave for this chicken a glasse that all menne may see in yt whatsoever they will and then saie certaine orations and praiers and so departe.   The third daie after digge up the spotte & you shall finde a glasse, which before any Bodie looke therin laie yt up for a 7 daies in a secret place and everie daie saie certain orations and so departe.   And the 7 daie take it awaie and thou shalle see in yt what thou will.

In another MS.* more reliance is placed on spells :

The manner to shut a spirit into a christall stone that will show thee anything thou desirest. Provide a cleare cristall stone and wrap him in virgin Parchment and wright on the backside of the   Parchment + Ossimmilis + Orebon + Malcalice + Askariel + Baylon + Offriel + Cosciel + Taketh + Bariel, and uppon the side that the stone is wrapped in wright + Cerberus + Chimfogro + Frodissma +

* 3851, 93 b.

Hundalgunda + Memibolo + Jamandundiceth + Lundemagnusa + Then say presently wrapping the stone within the parchment as followeth. [Then follows a prayer.]

A good deal of mediæval scrying had a very practical purpose—the discovering of stolen goods. A seventeenth-century MS. (Sloane 3849, f. 4 b) gives certain exhortations which you must repeat :

Let the chyld name them by these names sainge antor, anasor, anelor, shew mee the persons and the aparell of them that hath such a man's mony to this child and he will declare the person or persons and the apparell of them that had such a man's mony and if the come not the first day folow still to the chilld untill you may have a sight of them for the will apeare personalie as the to be knowne and the will declare how much of the mony is spent and how much is unspent.

And the feror day the better and let the child sit with his face toward the sune lookinge in the christal and ever ask him what hee seeth as youreade.

In other cases he object was to find lost friends : *

You angells of God, there is a friend of mine caled A. B. of C. in the country of D., that I have not seene nor heard of a long time. Tell us ye angells of God how he doth whether he bee in health or not, or

* 3851, f. 41 b.

whether he be dead or alive. Then they will tell you. Then you may say, you angells of God, shew us the said A.B. and what he is doing, whether he be in House of field or in what place he is, and what he is now doing. Shew us the truth in the name of Jesus. Then they will shew you. But they will name no place except you name it first : Therefore make your demands then, you angells of God, tell us truly in the name of the holy and blessed Trinitie how farr it is of the place where this A. B. is. Is it 5, 6, 7, 8, 10, 20 miles of. Tell us in the name of God. Then they will tell you. Then say, is it east, west, north, or south from this place ; then they will tell you. Then say, is it such a place. They will answer, it is or it is not. If they say, it is not, name some other place. They will show the childe the towne, house, signe if it have any, the very roome and what furniture, pickers etc. is in the roome, and what else you will demaund.

In others, again, the object was to compel runaways to come back : *

To cause one that is run away to returne. Seek out the said A. B. wheresoever he shall be uppon the face of the earth. Thou shalt haunt him, vex him, and torment him with such ougly odious fearfull and dreadfull sights and apparitions as if twenty divells in the likeness of Ramping lyons or Roring Bears were always haunting and following him as if they were carrying him away with such horrible fearfull and dreadfull hauntings that no creature is able to indure or behold.

Astrology seems to have mated itself with crystal gazing in some cases. Thus we find a MS. in the British Museum, written early in the seventeenth century by a certain "Arthur Gauntlet, who practised physick, and lived in Gray's Inn Lane." He says * :

Whosoever hath the following figure and shall use the invocation presently shall Oberion come in likeness of a beautifull man like a soldier personally in the ayre or in a glasse.

The first day of the Moone increasing and ascending when she shall be strong in the hour of ☽, take a sheete of ledd or of silver and the graven image of the foresaid spirit and his signe above his head and his name on his forehead, and the signe of the ☉ in the right part about the arme and the name of the angell of the ☉, which is Scorax, and the signe of the ☽ in the left parte and the name of the angell of the ☽ which is Carmelion.

[Here follows invocation.]

To appear in the ayre in the likeness of a boy of 7 years of age.

* 3851, f. 115 b.

We shall see later that incantation forms an important part of the ceremonies in Egyptian scrying. The reason of these long invocations and charms is not far to seek, especially if they are recited or sung, as stated by one of the authors to be quoted in the next chapter. The monotonous voice of a dull speaker has a notoriously soporific effect, which is due as much to the absence of modulation as to the lack of interest in the matter. The hypnotist, too, who uses the method of verbal suggestion, keeps his voice subdued, and on the same note.

We need not invariably suspect hypnotic influence (Mr Lang, indeed, denies that hypnotism has any connection with crystal gazing but he has probably not read the Egyptian cases). There can be little doubt that the good scryer is in an absolutely normal state in many cases. But there is equally little doubt that he or she is often drowsy. When there is no hypnotic influence the " charm " consists in distracting the scryer's attention, so that the reflections are not too obvious. This, in hypnotism, is the *raison d'être* of the invocation or " call."

CHAPTER VIII

EGYPTIAN SCRYING

Experiments by Lane—Lord Lindsay—Lord Nugent —Kinglake—Miss Martineau

THE most famous experiments in Egyptian magic are those of which Lane has given an account. At the time he was fully convinced of their supernormal character; but subsequently he revised his opinion, and was disposed, though with how much justice may be questioned, to lay all the successes at the door of a renegade Scotsman who officiated as interpreter.

" In preparing for the experiment of the magic mirror of ink, which, like some other performances of a similar nature, is here termed " darb elmendel," the magician first asked me for a reed-pen and ink, a piece of paper, and a pair of scissors—and, having cut off a narrow strip of paper, wrote upon it certain forms of invocation, together with another charm, by which he professes to accomplish the object of the experiment. He did not attempt to conceal these ; and on my asking him to give me copies of them, he readily consented, and immediately wrote them for me—explaining to me, at the same

time, that the object he had in view was accomplished through the influence of the first two words
—" Tarshun " and " Taryooshun " *—which, he
said, were the names of two genii—his " familiar
spirits." I compared the copies with the originals,
and found that they exactly agreed. Facsimiles
of them are here inserted, with a translation.

طرش طريونش انزلوا
انزلوا احضروا اى مذهب
الا مير وجنوده الى الاحمر
الا مير وجنوده احضروا
ما خدام هذه الاسماء

Magic invocation and charm:

Tarshun, Taryooshun. Come down.
Come down. Whither are gone
the prince and his troops? Where are El-
Ahmar
the prince and his troops? Be present
ye servants of these names.

* Or, " Tarsh " and " Taryoosh " — the final " un " being
the inflection which denotes the nominative case.

And this is the removal :

وهذا الاكشف فكشفنا عنك
غطاءك فبصرك اليوم
حديد صح صح

And we have removed from thee
thy veil ; and thy sight to-day
is piercing. Correct : correct.

Having written these the magician cut off the
paper containing the forms of invocation from that
upon which the other charm was written, and cut
the former into six strips. He then explained to
me the object of the latter charm (which contains
part of the twenty - first verse of the Soorat Kaf,
or fiftieth chapter of the Kur-an) was to open
the boy's eyes in a supernatural manner ; to make
his sight pierce into what is to us the invisible
world.

I had prepared, by the magician's direction, some
frankincense and coriander seed,* and a chafing-
dish with some live charcoal in it.

* He generally requires some benzoin to be added to these.

These were now brought into the room, together with the boy who was to be employed ; he had been called in, by my desire, from among some boys in the street, returning from a manufactory, and was about eight or nine years of age. In reply to my inquiry respecting the description of persons who could see in the magic mirror of ink, the magician said that they were a boy not arrived at puberty, a virgin, a black female slave, and a pregnant woman. The chafing-dish was placed before him and the boy, and the latter was placed on a seat.

The magician now desired my servant to put some frankincense and coriander seed into the chafing-dish ; then, taking hold of the boy's right hand, he drew, in the palm of it, a magic square, of which a copy is here given. (Plate III., figure 3). The figures which it contains are Arabic numerals.*   In the centre he poured

† The numbers in this magic square, in our own ordinary characters, are as follows :—

4	9	2
3	5	7
8	1	6

It will be seen that the horizontal, vertical, and diagonal rows give each the same sum—namely, 15.

G

a little ink, and desired the boy to look into it, and tell him if he could see his face reflected in it : the boy replied that he saw his face clearly. The magician, holding the boy's hand all the while,* told him to continue looking intently into the ink, and not to raise his head.

He then took one of the little strips of paper inscribed with the forms of invocation, and dropped it into the chafing-dish upon the burning coals and perfumes, which had already filled the room with their smoke, and as he did this he commenced an indistinct muttering of words, which he continued during the whole process, except when he had to ask the boy a question or to tell him what to say. The piece of paper containing the words from the Kuran he placed inside the forepart of the boy's takeeyeh, or skull-cap. He then asked him if he saw anything in the ink, and was answered: " No " ; but about a minute after the boy, trembling, and seeming much frightened, said : " I see a man sweeping the ground." " When he has done sweeping," said the magician, " tell me." Presently the boy said : " He has done." The magician then again interrupted his muttering to ask the boy if he knew what a " beyrak " (or flag) was, and being answered " Yes," desired him to say : " Bring a flag." The boy did so, and soon said : " He has brought a flag." " What colour is it ? " asked the

* This reminds us of animal magnetism.

magician. The boy replied: " Red." He was
told to call for another flag, which he did ; and soon
after he said that he saw another brought, and
that it was black. In like manner, he was told
to call for a third, fourth, fifth, sixth, and seventh,
which he described as being successively brought
before him, specifying their colours as white,
green, black, red, and blue. The magician then
asked him (as he did, also, each time that a new
flag was described as being brought): " How many
flags have you now before you?" "Seven," answered
the boy. While this was going on the magician
put the second and third of the small strips of paper
upon which the forms of invocation were written
into the chafing-dish, and fresh frankincense and
coriander seed having been added the fumes became painful to the eyes. When the boy had
described the seven flags as appearing to him he
was desired to say: " Bring the Sultan's tent, and
pitch it." This he did, and in about a minute after
he said: " They have set it up." " Now," said
the magician, " order the soldiers to come, and to
pitch their camp around the tent of the Sultan."
The boy did as he was desired, and immediately said:
" I see a great many soldiers with their tents ;
they have pitched their tents." He was then told
to order that the soldiers should be drawn up in
ranks, and having done so he presently said that
he saw them thus arranged. The magician had

put the fourth of the little strips of paper into the chafing-dish; and soon after he did the same with the fifth. He now said: "Tell some of the people to bring a bull." The boy gave the order required, and said: "I see a bull; it is red; four men are dragging it along, and three are beating it." He was told to desire them to kill it, and cut it up, and to put the meat into saucepans, and cook it. He did as he was directed, and described these operations as apparently performed before his eyes. "Tell the soldiers," said the magician, "to eat it." The boy did so, and said: "They are eating it. They have done, and are washing their hands." The magician then told him to call for the Sultan, and the boy having done this, said: "I see the Sultan riding to his tent on a bay horse, and he has on his head a high red cap; he has alighted at his tent, and sat down within it." "Desire them to bring coffee to the Sultan," said the magician, "and to form the court." These orders were given by the boy, and he said that he saw them performed. The magician had put the last of the little strips of paper into the chafing-dish. In his mutterings I distinguished nothing but the words of the written invocation, frequently repeated, except on two or three occasions, when I heard him say: "If they demand information inform them, and be ye veracious." But much that he repeated was inaudible, and as I did not ask him to teach me his art I do not pretend to assert that I am fully acquainted with his invocations.

He now addressed himself to me, and asked me if I wished the boy to see any person who was absent or dead. I named Lord Nelson, of whom the boy had evidently never heard, for it was with much difficulty that he pronounced the name, after several trials. The magician desired the boy to say to the Sultan : " My master salutes thee, and desires thee to bring Lord Nelson. Bring him before my eyes, that I may see him, speedily." The boy then said so, and almost immediately added : " A messenger is gone, and has returned, and brought a man, dressed in a black * suit of European clothes ; the man has lost his left arm." He then paused for a moment or two, and looking more intently and more closely into the ink, said : " No ; he has not lost his left arm, but it is placed to his breast." This correction made his description more striking than it had been without it, since Lord Nelson generally had his empty sleeve attached to the breast of his coat ; but it was the *right* arm that he had lost. Without saying that I suspected the boy had made a mistake I asked the magician whether the objects appeared in the ink as if actually before the eyes, or as in a glass, which makes the right appear

* Dark blue is called by the modern Egyptian "eswed," which properly signifies *black*, and is therefore so translated here.

left. He answered that they appeared as in a mirror. This rendered the boy's description faultless.

The next person I called for was a native of Egypt who had been for many years resident in England, where he had adopted our dress, and who had been confined to his bed by illness before I embarked for this country.* I thought that his name, one not very uncommon in Egypt, might make the boy describe him incorrectly ; though another boy, on the former visit of the magician, had described this same person as wearing a European dress like that in which I last saw him. In the present case the boy said : " Here is a man brought on a kind of bier, and wrapped up in a sheet." This description would suit, supposing the person in question to be still confined to his bed, or if he were dead.† The

---

* Whenever I desired the boy to call for any person to appear I paid particular attention both to the magician and to Osman. The latter gave no direction either by word or sign, and, indeed, he was generally unacquainted with the personal appearance of the individual called for. I took care that he had no previous communication with the boys, and have seen the experiment fail when he *could* have given directions to them or to the magician. In short, it would be difficult to conceive any precaution which I did not take. It is important to add that the dialect of the magician was more intelligible to me than to the boy. When *I* understood him perfectly at once he was sometimes obliged to vary his words to make the *boy* comprehend what he said. (In the *Quarterly*, lix. 201, Lane also states that he and the three mentioned in the text were the only persons present.)

† A few months after this was written I had the pleasure

boy described his face as covered, and was told to order that it should be uncovered. This he did ; and then said : " His face is pale, and he has moustaches, but no beard "—which is correct.

Several other persons were successively called for ; but the boy's descriptions of them were imperfect, though not altogether incorrect. He represented each object as appearing less distinct than the preceding one, as if his sight were gradually becoming dim ; he was a minute, or more, before he could give any account of the persons he professed to see towards the close of the performance, and the magician said it was useless to proceed with him. Another boy was then brought in, and the magic square, etc., made in his hand, but he could see nothing. The magician said he was too old.

Though completely puzzled, I was somewhat disappointed with his performances, for they fell short of what he had accomplished, in many instances, in presence of certain of my friends and countrymen. On one of these occasions an Englishman present ridiculed the performance, and said that nothing would satisfy him but a correct description of his father, of whom, he was sure, no one of the company had any knowledge. The boy,

of hearing that the person here alluded to was in better health. Whether he was confined to his bed at the time when this experiment was performed I have not been able to ascertain.

accordingly, having called by name for the person
alluded to, described a man in a Frank dress, with
his hand placed to his head, wearing spectacles, and
with one foot on the ground, and the other raised
behind him, as if he were stepping down from a
seat. The description was exactly true in every
respect : the peculiar position of the hand was
occasioned by an almost constant headache, and
that of the foot or leg by a stiff knee, caused by a
fall from a horse in hunting. I am assured that
on this occasion the boy accurately described each
person and thing called for. On another occasion
Shakespeare was described with the most minute
correctness, both as to person and dress ; and I
might add several other cases in which the same
magician had excited astonishment in the sober
minds of Englishmen of my acquaintance. A short
time since, after performing in the usual manner,
by means of a boy, he prepared the magic mirror
in the hand of a young English lady, who on looking
into it for a little while said that she saw a broom
sweeping the ground without anybody holding it,
and was so much frightened that she would look no
longer."

Lane was invited in 1844 to act as interpreter
for Lord Nugent at a trial with the magician. His
account was published by his sister,* and states
that two boys were tried, both of whom were com-

* *Englishwoman in Egypt,* ii. 163 *et seq.*

plete failures. The magician excused himself on the ground that the boys were liars, and did not describe what they really saw, adding that he was successful in the days of Osman Effendi, but had been unfortunate since his death.

Now, it so happens that Osman Effendi was the interpreter employed by the magician, and Lane says that in all the surprising successes of which he had heard this Osman had served in that capacity.

Subsequently, though hundreds of persons had gone to the magician, the successes had been so few that coincidence sufficed to explain them. (Lane says coincidence was *not* necessary to explain them, but obviously means that nothing more than chance had been at work.)

Lane goes on to say that though he was satisfied that the boys in his own case were not prompted by the magician, as he himself had selected them, yet he now believed that they had not in reality seen anything. He had, indeed, offered them a bribe to confess the truth, but they had remained silent, fearing to confess. (What they feared it is difficult to see.)

To the obvious objection that Europeans (as we shall see later) had succeeded in seeing things in the ink, Lane replies by propounding this hypothesis —sufficiently remarkable at a time when the efficacy of verbal suggestion was virtually unknown—that in their case it was the interpreter who helped them to accomplish their feats, and that he did it by means of suggestions. But if this explanation, by no means improbable, fits the case of the Europeans, it is difficult to see why Lane supposes the boys to have seen nothing.

If he had been prepared to go a little further, and admit that the boys frequently saw ink visions which were, in the main, or at any rate on some occasions, the result of suggestion on the part of the magician, he would probably have hit the mark.

An important point remains to be mentioned. The aforesaid Osman Effendi was in reality a Scotsman, an ex-soldier who had been taken prisoner in 1807, who had gone over to Mohammedanism, and subsequently become second interpreter at the British Consulate.* His avowed theory of morals was that " we did our whole duty if we did what we thought best for our fellow-creatures and most agreeable to them "—a doctrine which has more than once been put into practice by friends of my own in reporting their psychical experiences to me.

It is, therefore, highly probable that Osman was acquainted with the appearance of a good many celebrated Englishmen, including, of course, Nelson. Lane was astonished to hear an accurate description of Burckhardt, knowing that the magician had never seen him. But perhaps the mystery vanishes

* Nugent, *Lands Classical*, i. 249.

when we hear that Burckhardt had been Osman's patron. Osman had also known well the gentleman described to Lane as lying on a sofa ; he had even, Lane believed, inquired about his health, and been told that he was suffering from rheumatism. It is, therefore, small wonder if the boy described him as lying on a sofa and looking ill.

Though the facts just disclosed throw grave doubts on the cases of Nelson, Shakespeare, and others, with whose appearance Osman would probably, or possibly, have been familiar, there remains a good deal of evidence in favour of veridical scrying, as we shall see in the next chapter. It must not be forgotten that Lane in his earlier narrative asserts most positively that collusion was impossible, and that Osman held no communication with the boy ; while the magician, who, perhaps, was hardly likely to have crammed descriptions of English celebrities, for his part did *not* seize the opportunity of cheating when it was possible for him to do so.

On the other hand, the numerous failures recorded by European observers, and admitted, if Lane's account is correct, by the magician, tell strongly against the telepathic theory. For it is difficult to see how Osman's presence could have helped thought transference between the Arab urchin and the European observer. As example of these failures we may quote the following.

Lord Lindsay had previously heard of the magician's performances, and was determined to test him. On the second occasion he was alone, and the magician is said to have failed egregiously— only one trial, and that the first, being successful.*

The process of becoming a magician was, it appeared, somewhat complicated. Thirteen words or names, apparently not Arabic, had to be learnt by heart; then for seven days a fire must be made seven times a day, and incense thrown on it. Round this fire the initiant had to walk seven times, pronouncing seven times the thirteen names (it reminds one of the man who was going to St Ives), and then go to sleep, to wake with the desired faculty.

Before the boy was brought the magician wrote several lines in Arabic, which he afterwards tore into seven pieces, each containing a distich.

He then drew a double-lined square, with strange marks in the angles, on the boy's hand, put ink on his palm, and bade him look in.

A chafing-dish was now brought in, and the wizard, beads in hand, began mumbling prayers or invocations, probably the same words over and over again, at first in a loud voice, then sinking it till it was quite inaudible, though his lips continued to move. From time to time he placed incense and one of the scraps of paper on the fire, frequently

* Lord Lindsay, *Letters*, p. 65.

breaking off to ask the boy if he saw anything.
At last he said : " I saw something flit by quickly " ;
but nothing more came, and the wizard asked for
another boy.

After a repetition of the ceremonies the new boy
saw a man, who at the word of command began
sweeping ; then he made the boy call for seven
flags in succession, which made their appearance,
and finally the Sultan, who was described as drinking
coffee. " Now," said the magician, " the charm is
complete, and you may call for anyone you like."

The first person summoned, a clergyman, whose
name is not given, was, on the whole, accurately
described, but this was the only success. The
others would not come, or appeared by proxy—a
result which, with an ingenuity which has its
parallel nearer home, the magician ascribed to the
fact that it was the month of Ramadan.

Daniel Lambert appeared as a scarecrow, and
Miss Biffin a legless and armless freak, with the
usual number of human properties. In spite of
failures, Lord Lindsay was satisfied that the children
did see crowds of objects, and that collusion was
out of the question.

Lord Nugent gives a brief description of two
seances, the second being the one at which Lane
was present. At the first, after the usual incense-
burning, the magician placed a paper with some

written characters under the cap of the boy, who had been brought from a distance by Sir Gardner Wilkinson. The preliminary pictures were, in the main, the same as those already described—persons pitching a tent, a man sweeping, spreading a carpet, etc. After this preparation the inquirers were asked to name their fancy, and selected a person distinguished for the longest and bushiest beard in the British Isles. He was, however, described as having a chin very like that of the youngest person in the company, Lord Mountcharles. After several failures the magician suggested that they should ask for someone who had lost a limb, as they be more easily recognised. Sir Henry Hardinge was selected, and the boy, after being led astray by inquiries after his eyes and feet, mentioned that he had his hands crossed on his heart—the real fact being that he had lost one of them, which led O'Connell to abuse him in Parliament as a "one-handed miscreant." The second seance was likewise a total failure.*

Kinglake's curiosity was aroused by the reports of the magician's feats, and he had a seance; † but the result was a lamentable failure. Dr Keate, the headmaster of Eton, was described as a fair girl, with blue eyes, golden hair, pallid face, and rosy lips.

Miss Martineau's scryer was equally unsuccessful.‡

* *Lands Classical*, p. 227.   † *Eothen*, p. 264.   ‡ *Travels*, ii. 137.

As a subject she showed signs of getting results,
but got alarmed, and broke off the experiment.
She says that the magician did not come the first
time. On the second occasion, kind treatment
and special attention having been promised him,
he made his appearance, and as interpreter Stanley
Lane Poole, but all the experiments were failures.

The Arab boy had been brought by the magician
himself, or at any rate he was not selected by any
one of the investigators. He crouched close to the
magician and his pans of charcoal, the incense
from which was so powerful that three of the party,
in spite of their promise of special attention, were
soon fast asleep. Miss Martineau, who had no sense
of smell, was unaffected, and consequently her
narrative, she suggests, is not open to the objection
that she was hallucinated.

As soon as the old man had poured the ink into
the boy's hand, and had his own left hand at liberty,
he rested the tips of the fingers firmly on the crown
of the boy's head, and kept them there. He explained that he did so in order that the boy might
look fixedly at the ink; but Miss Martineau mentions
that he did so to none of the others who were brought
in, nor to herself, when she afterwards became the
subject of the experiment. The eyelids of the boy
were observed to quiver in a way that Miss Martineau
regarded as " characteristic of a mesmeric subject."

She came to the conclusion that the whole matter

was an affair of "mesmerism"; in the first place, a clairvoyant got *en rapport* with the questioner, and succeeded in answering correctly. The magician, she thought, failed to appreciate the cause of his success, and attributed it to the favour of the spirits whom he propitiated.

After several more boys had turned out failures, Miss Martineau proposed to try for herself. At first the magician objected, but subsequently agreed to her request, though with a warning that success was improbable.

" More charms and incense were burned," she goes on," my hand was duly scored with ink, and the usual pool poured into my hand, and I faithfully gazed into it. In two minutes the sensation came, though there was no hand on my head. . . . Presently I began to see such odd things in the pool of ink ; it grew so large before my aching eyes, and showed such strange moving shadows and clear symmetrical figures and intersecting lines, that I felt uncertain how long I could command my thoughts and words ; and, considering the number of strangers present, I thought it more prudent to shake off the influence while I could than to pursue the experiment. The perfumes might have some effect, though I was insensible to them. . . . I am certain that there was a strong mesmeric influence present."

CHAPTER IX

Laborde's account—Quarterly Review—*A. J. Butler*

A LONG account of Egyptian magicians is given by Laborde,* who was in Cairo in 1827, and witnessed a seance at Lord Prudhoe's. After a description of the man, an Algerian, he states that two boys were brought in, not, apparently, by Achmed—one of whom, the first selected, was the son of a European, and eleven years old. He spoke Arabic with ease.

The magician, noticing that he seemed alarmed, calmed his apprehensions, and proceeded to inscribe on his hand with a pen a square with letters and numbers. Then he poured ink into the middle, and told the boy to look at his own reflection. He next asked for a pan of charcoal, and threw various ingredients on the fire, and finally told the boy to tell him when he saw a Turkish soldier sweeping. Thereupon he recited a quantity of Arabic in a low voice, which he gradually raised, though few words were intelligible to his audience, seated in a circle round him.

The boy kept his eyes fixed on the ink, and the

* Laborde, *Commentaire*, p. 23.

odour of incense grew stronger. All at once, throwing back his head, the boy burst into tears, and declared he had seen a hideous figure.

Thereupon a little Arab, attached to the house, who had never seen Achmed, took the first boy's place, and after the same preliminaries he cried, all at once: " There he is." Thereupon Achmed questioned him, and in the description we find an account of a soldier sweeping before a richly-orna-mented tent, of the appearance of the Sultan, his suite, and so on—a narrative so detailed that Laborde concludes that the boy must have been de-scribing what he saw. Thereupon the magician asked the company to select someone who should appear, and Major Felix selected Shakespeare. " Bring Shakespeare," cried the magician, and proceeded to repeat various unintelligible formulas. The boy described him as dressed in black, with a beard, and a black *benisch*, or cloak. In reply to a question as to where he was born the company were told: " In a country surrounded by water."

Lord Prudhoe then called for Cradock, who was described as dressed in red, with odd boots, and a great black *tarbousch* (cocked hat) on his head ; the boots were such as the boy had never seen, and came over his legs.

According to Laborde, the beard attributed to Shakespeare was a detail that the boy could hardly have invented, inasmuch as it was not worn by the Europeans with European dress whom he had seen. Mr Cradock, who was on an embassy to the Pacha, was likewise attired in an unusual costume. Laborde therefore concluded that the boy really saw what he described, the more so as the boy hesitated in his description from a lack of words to express what he saw.

After several more people had been summoned and described the child appeared fatigued. Achmed therefore raised his head, and applied his thumbs to his eyes, reciting prayers, and there left him. The boy appeared as if drunk, his forehead covered with perspiration, and his eyes with the unsteady look and roll of the inebriate's.

Laborde, who was suspicious of a mystification, authorised his dragoman, Bellin, to buy the secret from Achmed, undertaking to keep silence on the matter as long as the magician lived. As soon as the company retired Laborde learnt that the magician consented, and that he would receive a lesson in magic on the following day. On reaching Achmed's house Laborde found that his journey had been in vain, but a second attempt was more successful. For thirty piastres the magician undertook to communicate the secret, provided he took an oath on the Koran to keep silence. This settled, he traced on a piece of paper the characters to be inscribed on the hand, and Laborde wrote the spell at his dictation: Anzilon — Aiouha — el - Djenni —

Aiouha — el Djennoun — Anzilon — Betakki —
Metalahoutouhou — Aleikoum — Taricki, Anzilon,
Taricki.

The words are not difficult, but they must, it
appears, be recited or sung in a certain way, and
with certain repetitions. The incense was composed of Takeh-Mabachi, Ambar-Indi, and Kon-
sombra-Djaou—equal quantities of the first two and
less of the third.

As soon as Laborde reached home he set to work
to practise his spells, and soon attained the proper
tone and rhythmic cadence. A few days after
learning the secret he was called by business to
Alexandria, and went by boat, on which, to the
great admiration of his crew, he made two successful
experiments. At Alexandria, his suspicions of
Achmed still active, he went into remote quarters
of the city to find boys on whom to experiment,
and brought them in from highways and byways.
Only one experiment is, however, mentioned—in
which he asked for Lord Prudhoe. The boy described his costume exactly, and added that he had
a silver sabre, the fact being that he had a sheath
of that metal, probably the only one in Egypt.

On his return to Cairo, Laborde found his reputation had procured him clients. The servants of M.
Massara, dragoman of the French Consulate, came
to enlist his aid in tracing a thief. He sent them
out to fetch a child ; and we may assume that he was

not an accomplice, for, to Laborde's dismay, the
vision refused to develop. At last the caouas
appeared, and the thief was demanded. The boy
gave a description of his face, his turban, his beard,
and so on, leaving no doubt on Laborde's mind
that he was really describing a picture. The Arabs
were equally sure that they recognised the male-
factor, and left without more ado, with a few remarks
as to the benefits that result from a few applications
of the rod.

Proud of his success Laborde wished to buy other
secrets from Achmed, but learnt that he was dead,
and had, in fact, suffered decapitation as a result of
an unfortunate overdose of a medicament sought
by an old Turk who wished to renew his youth.

From Lane's account it appears that Laborde
was wrong in thinking that Achmed, whom Lane
calls Cheich-Abd-el-Kader-el-Mougreby, was dead.
He had merely suffered banishment.

The *Quarterly* * supplies a commentary to the
earlier part of this narrative.

An eye-witness says : " That the boy really sees
what he describes is evident. . . . The ink is about
half a teaspoonful."

" De Laborde's account is inaccurate. The scene
was described more than once to the writer by people
who had been present. The first boy was the son
of an Italian merchant ; he saw his cap, then his

nose, and finally burst into tears at the sight of a man with a sword. The son of M. Massara was more successful. De Laborde asked for the Duc de la Rivière, without telling anyone of his intention, and the boy described him as having a uniform, with silver lace on the cuffs and collar. This was the uniform of the Grand Veneur, and the Duke was the only person in France who had such a uniform. An interesting point in this experiment was that the boy heard the Sultan (who was always present) send for the Duke ; he said he saw his lips move, and heard the words in his ear.

When Shakespeare was sent for the boy burst into a laugh, and explained that he saw a man with a beard under his lip instead of on his chin, with a *candeel* (a tumbler-shaped glass lamp) upside-down on his head ; the man lived on an island."

The account states that "the boy frequently sat at a distance from the magician, and he sometimes went to another part of the room while the child described the figures." *

A further contribution is supplied by Christopher North.† In "Noctes Ambrosianæ" an account is given of the interview, stated to have taken place in 1830, between Lord Prudhoe, Major Felix, and the magician. The latter told him to fetch a boy. After walking about for half-an-hour they selected one about eight years old. After the usual incantation he saw a horseman, then several, then the Sultan. Thereupon the guests were asked to say who should be described. One of them named Shakespeare, and the boy described " a pale-faced Frank—but not dressed like these Franks—with large eyes, a pointed beard, a tall hat, roses on his shoes, and a short mantle." Voltaire was the next, and was said to be " a lean, old, yellow-faced Frank, with a huge brown wig, a nutmeg-grater profile, spindle shanks, buckled shoes, and a gold snuff-box." Then Lord Prudhoe named Archibald Wrangham, and the Arab boy said : " I perceive a tall, grey-haired Frank, with a black silk petticoat, walking in a garden, with a little book in his hand. He is reading in the book ; his eyes are bright and gleaming, his teeth are white ; he is the happiest-looking Frank I ever beheld."

A more recent narrative is that of A. J. Butler.* One day Butler, who was tutor to the Khedive's sons, heard from him the following story :—" A Turk in Cairo had a ring with a red stone, said to have come from Mecca, and a plate of silver with verses from the Koran engraved on it. He could not work the charm himself, but required the presence of a child under ten years of age. The child took the ring, the silver plate was put on its head, and in a little while the colour of the stone changed to white. Thereupon the child looked

* Butler, *Court Life*, 238 *et seq.*

into it, and saw visions." Such was the account given by the Khedive.

He went on to say that, being quite incredulous, he asked permission to make a private trial at home. The owner consented, and at the Ismailia Palace a little girl eight years old, the child of a nurse, quite ignorant, and unable to read or write, was selected. When the plate was put on her head she cried out : " The stone has turned to white." Thereupon the Khedive asked questions about people whom the child had not seen, and received correct descriptions. Another person present asked : " How many children have I ? "

" Two sons and a daughter."

" That is right.   What is the elder son like ? "

" He wears a coat with a row of buttons down the front, and striped trousers, and has a sabre."

" What is the second son like ? "

" He has a coat with two rows of buttons in front, little gold cushions on his shoulders, and an anchor embroidered on his cuffs."

One was in the Turkish army, the other in the Turkish navy, and both were absolutely unknown to the child. Collusion was impossible, for even a wizard would find it hard to penetrate into the ladies' apartments of the Khedive's palace. Moreover, the questions were too rapid and too varied to admit of shuffling.

Butler says that the story was subsequently told

in French in his presence, and that the second version was absolutely the same. The Khedive attempted to get the ring for further experiments in Butler's presence, but the owner, Ahmed Agha, would not be persuaded. Subsequently Butler was unable to find him, but learnt that he had made a reputation for curing people of rheumatism by sticking needles into the affected part. No blood flowed, and no pain was inflicted.

On the whole, the narratives in this chapter go far to rehabilitate Egyptian magic. If Osman were the *deus ex machina* in the case of Nelson and Shakespeare we can hardly suppose him to have been intimately acquainted with the appearance of Voltaire. It may be said that he " got up " descriptions; but there remain Archdeacon Wrangham and the Duc de la Rivière, and Osman Effendi could hardly have " got up " their personal appearance, even if he had known beforehand that they would be asked for. More convincing than all, there is the description of Lord Prudhoe given by the street urchin of Alexandria, far from the renegade Scots private's baneful influence.

The more recent experiments described by Butler, told at second-hand, however, point in the same direction.

CHAPTER X

PROPHETIC AND TELEPATHIC SCRYING

Catherine de Medici—Duc d'Orleans—Mrs B.'s mother's mayde—Thief-catching in Egypt

IN the historical and ethnographical chapters we have seen more than one hint of the reasons which made the crystal and similar visions so popular— their telepathic, or alleged telepathic, character. Savage scryer and civilised crystal gazer both allege that by the use of the crystal they are enabled to discover events which are happening at a distance, and some even claim that their visions give them the means of foretelling the future.

In the volume on thought transference we have seen what minute precautions are necessary in order to make the experiments evidentially valuable. In the nature of things, the spontaneous thought transference, which is, as a rule, all that seems to be attained by crystal gazing, is less susceptible of rigid control, for the simple reason that the scryer is seldom able to see the person for whom he or she is looking, and that even where this does not hold good, and the person asked for appears in the crystal, steps have but seldom been taken, in the cases actually recorded, to get from the subject of the vision a contemporaneous account of his or her proceedings.

It is true that there is, as a rule, but little reason to distrust the *post facto* statements of the unconscious parties to the experiments, if in asking for details corroborative of the vision the inquirer is (as he should be) extremely careful not to suggest the answer for which he is looking, if, perchance, he regards the scry as *prima facie* telepathic. But, when all is said and done, the evidence is necessarily of a more rough and ready character than that for experimental thought transference, and is, further, incapable of statistical treatment.

Numerous though the reports of telepathic and other supernormal cases are in the literature of the subject, much caution is needed, especially in dealing with older accounts.

Catherine de Medici is said to have consulted a magician in the Castle of Chaumont in order to see if her children would succeed to the throne. According to Pasquier,* she was shown into a room, and the magician then drew a circle, outside of which appeared all the kings of France that had been and that were to be, and they walked round the room once for each year of their reign. It appears, however, that the vision, if it were a vision, only included those who had already reigned, for it ceased

* *Lettres,* p. 20.

at Henri IV. And we may have grave doubts, the scene being the residence of the magician, whether a certain number of his servants, dressed up, did not play the parts of the kings of France.

As an illustration of how such stories grow, we way quote the account of another author,* who assures us that Catherine de Medici made use of the magic of her diviners to learn who would succeed her son, and that by means of a mirror she was shown all future kings, beginning from Henri IV. She saw after him Louis XIII., Louis XIV., and then a troop of Jesuits; whereupon she refused to see more, and was on the point of breaking the mirror, which, however, was said to be preserved in the Louvre.

The only point of resemblance between the two stories is that Henri IV. appeared in each, and that as soon as the king appeared who was actually reigning at the time the work quoted was published Catherine refused to see more ; even the scene of the event is changed to the Louvre.   The story is, perhaps, entirely fabulous, or at any rate non-evidential.†

Saint Simon ‡ gives an account of a professedly prophetic vision.

* *Remarques sur le Gouvernement*, Cologne, 1688, p. 15.

† For a discussion of a recent mirror vision of great interest see p. 148.

‡ Saint Simon, *Mem.* v. 120,

The Duc d'Orleans related to him in 1706, the day after the event, that visions had been shown by someone in a glass of water at Madame de Sery's. Wishing to test this, he sent a valet to Madame de Nancie's to see who was there, and so on. As soon as the Duke got his information he asked the little girl of eight, who was the scryer, to say what was going on. She related everything exactly. To make sure, M. de Nancie was despatched, and he confirmed the exactness of the description.

Then the Duke asked for a description of Versailles, which she had never seen, nor heard of anyone belonging to the Court. She described the King's room, Madame de Maintenon, Fagon, the Duchess of Orleans, the Princess of Conti. The King himself, the Dukes of Berry and Bourgogne, and the Duchess of Bourgogne, she did not describe.

The Duke had wished to see the future, and especially the events at the death of the King; and Saint Simon remarks that the three persons mentioned died before the King.

A MS.* in the British Museum gives some particulars derived by the writer from a certain Mrs Bollsworth:

1. Mrs B.'s mother had a Mayd who (when her mistress was abroad) was busy in an arbor in ye garden, whom Mrs B., being then a girle, found

* *Eg.* 2618.

looking in a Copper-basin with water in it,* and she looking into it [as ye mayd wished her] spied something quite thro' it, as if it had been a glass & saw (as if it was) the shape of a great numb. of men fighting one with another—which after was judged to be ye representation of Worcester fight, it being at that time for ye Mayd told Her Mistress and all in ye House the same night or day after it was fought, telling the Kngs. party was worsted and several particulars of the fight, wh. she saw and learned in that basin.

2. A 2d trick of this mayde to wch. Mrs B. was a witness was her showing a Gentleman his Mistress in a Comon looking glass belonging to ye house, putting behind it a paper with barbarous words and characters on it. She bid the Gentleman whose name was . . . & 2 or 3 more (with that Mrs Bollsw.) to look in it and they all (as they said in Mrs B.'s hearing) and she particularly for herself averred that she saw a Gentlewoman very distinctly in ye glass in the daytime, picking her teeth wch. the Gentleman confessed was his very Mistress.

They desired ye mayd to show her again in ye Afternoon, wch Mrs B. and ye reste saw again in another posture with a book in her hand and sitting

---

* With a copper basin with water in it, often throwing it out yt ye water might be clear. Mrs B. having heard she was a witch was curious to see ye event of ye thing : ye mayd was unwilling at first but at last Mrs B. would look into ye basin.

in a coach. This Gent. after asking his lady her postures and business those 2 times, she confesst it was true what they saw.

3. A young woman known in ye family desired Bess (ye mayd's name) to show her her sweetheart, wch she did in ye looking glass, showing a man under ye barber's hand, who starting up suddenly, his face seemed bloody. This Mrs B. saw very plainly with ye rest of ye company : upon enquiry ye Gentl. was at that first (?) time found to have been cut by a barber and rose up hastily.*

Mr B. also heard ye particulars of this same story from ye s^d gentlewoman (*sic*) as well as from his wife 30 years ago.

4. Mrs B. saw another time in ye glass several shapes and psons as ye sea and a ship and one remarkable pson in ye ship leaning on his elbow (wch some of ye company there said was King Charles) this before his restoracon.

This Mr B. also heard long ago from his wife and from others who saw it as well as she but Bess could never raise up Oliver.

5. Mrs B. saw several other times but less perfect shapes. Bess would let nobody stand behind the glass.

Afterwards several people came to know their fortunes and find lost things.

* She showed ye same Gentl. afterwards in the glass with a patch on.

These particulars to me June 24, 1691.

W. SHIPPON.

We cannot, however, lay stress on narratives of this sort, which reach us at second-hand, and without any guarantee that the reporter recorded the facts while they were fresh in his memory. It is hardly open to question that the second-hand story tends to undergo greater changes when it is recorded after a certain lapse of time than the narrative which is given us at first-hand. This is readily intelligible ; the memories of the second-hand reporter are far more likely to rearrange themselves so as to produce a good story, and the recollection of the original narrative, which is all he has to go by, is little check on the mythopœic faculty of the ordinary man.

Some first-hand cases, *prima facie* telepathic, are rendered valueless by the failure of the recorder to exclude commonplace explanations. In the following Indian case there is nothing to show that the dog-boy was not the thief or that the real thief did not confess. Possibly the wizard himself hid the objects where they were subsequently found :—

Having had some property stolen I sent for a Lubbi jadugon, or wizard, who promised to recover it, and chose my dog-boy, a lad of eleven years, as

his confederate.   After some preliminary incantation the boy was asked what he saw in the globule.*
He first described the inside of a tent, then said he
saw monkeys sweeping the room, and after gazing
intently on the globule for some minutes got
frightened at something, and began to cry.   The
Lubbi on this led him from the room, returned in
half-an-hour, and informed me the missing articles
were under a chest of drawers in my bedroom,
which proved to be the case. †

In other cases we find the witnesses disagreeing
on important points.   Thus in the story told by
Lane of the detection of a thief by an Egyptian
magician an Arab boy is the scryer, and the thief
is, apparently, an Arab too.   The account is, if not
contemporary, at anyrate written within five or six
years of the occurrence.

Dr Wolff, who was one of the party, gives no account, so far as I have been able to ascertain, in his
contemporary journals.   His travels, however,
published thirty years later, contain a very striking
account of the incident.   Lane, it is true, may have
had an inaccurate account given him, or the story
may have faded in his memory, but the discrepancy
is remarkable.   For in Wolff's narrative the scryer
is not an Arab at all but an Italian, and the thief,

* Unjun, a shiny globule, is made of castor oil and lamp-
black.

† *N. and Q.* 3rd S., xi. 180.

I

to judge by his name, was an Italian too. It may be noted that if Wolff's account is accurate very much more turns on the closeness of the resemblance. For an Italian boy would be likely to see an Italian, and the racial resemblance might be enough to procure recognition. Lane's account is as follows :—

A few days after my first arrival in this country my curiosity was excited on the subject of magic by a circumstance related to me by Mr Salt, our Consul-General. Having had reason to believe that one of his servants was a thief, from the fact of several articles of property having been stolen from his house, he sent for a celebrated Maghrabee magician, with a view of intimidating them, and causing the guilty one (if any of them were guilty) to confess his crime. The magician came, and said that he would cause the exact image of the person who had committed the thefts to appear to any youth not arrived at the age of puberty, and desired the master of the house to call in any boy whom he might choose. As several boys were then employed in a garden adjacent to the house, one of them was called for this purpose. In the palm of the boy's right hand the magician drew with a pen a certain diagram, in the centre of which he poured a little ink. Into this ink he desired the boy steadfastly to look. He then burned some incense and several bits of paper inscribed with charms, and at the same time called for various objects to appear in the ink. The boy declared that he saw all these objects, and, last of all, the image of the guilty person ; he described his stature, countenance, and dress ; said that he knew him ; and directly ran down into the garden, and apprehended one of the labourers, who, when brought before the master, immediately confessed that he was the thief. . . .*

Wolff gives some details :

He was sitting one day at the table of Mr Salt, dining with

---

* Lane's *Modern Egyptians*, 1871, vol. i. p. 337.

him. The guests who were invited were as follows :—Bokhti, the Swedish Consul-General, a nasty atheist and infidel ; Major Ross of Ronturn, in Ireland, a gentleman in every respect, and highly principled ; Wolff himself, and Caviglia, who was the only believer in magic there. Salt began to say : " . . . I wish to know who has stolen a dozen of my silver spoons, a dozen forks, and a dozen knives." C. said : " If you want to know you must send for the magician." Osman, the interpreter, fetched him, but he insists on postponing his trial. " I will come again to-morrow at noon, before which time you must either have procured a woman with child or a boy seven years of age—either of whom will tell who has been the thief." Bokhti, the scoffing infidel, . . . said : " I am determined to unmask imposture, and therefore I shall bring, to-morrow, a boy who is not quite seven years of age, and who came a week ago from Leghorn. He has not stirred out of my house, nor does he know anybody, nor is he known to anybody, and he does not speak Arabic ; him I will bring with me for the magician." The boy came at the time appointed, and all the party were again present, when the magician entered with a large pan in his hand, into which he poured some black colour, and mumbled some unintelligible words ; and then he said to the boy : " Stretch out your hands." He said this in Arabic, which the boy did not understand. But Wolff interpreted what the magician had said, and then the boy stretched out his hands flat, when the magician put some of the black colour upon his palm, and said to him : " Do you see something ? " which was interpreted to the lad. The boy coolly, in his Italian manner, shrugged his shoulders, and replied : " Vedo niente." Again the magician poured the coloured liquid into his hand, and mumbled some words, and asked the boy again : " Do you see something ? " And the boy said the second time : " I see nothing." Then the magician poured the colour into the hand a third time, and inquired :, " Do you see something ? " On which the boy suddenly exclaimed, and it made every one of us turn pale, and tremble in both knees, as if we were paralysed : " Io vedo un uomo." The fourth time the stuff was poured into his hand, and the boy loudly screamed out : " Io vedo un uomo con un capello." And, in short, after a dozen times of inquiry, he described the man so minutely that all present exclaimed : " Salvini is the thief." And when Salvini's room was searched the silver spoons, etc., were found. No one except the boy saw anything.*

The case is obviously of little value from an evidential point of view.

* Wolff, *Travels*, 118.

CHAPTER XI

EVIDENTIAL CASES

Miss A—Premonitions—Miss Gernet—Mr Lang's cases—Collective scrying

In F. W. H. Myers' great series of papers on the subliminal consciousness is an interesting account of some of the crystal visions of the lady known as Miss A, which form but a small portion of those which she has actually seen—the crystal visions being again but a fraction of the supernormal phenomena recorded in connection with her.

The records are, it may be noted, incomplete, mainly because they were not made with a view to their use for scientific purposes. For the same reason they naturally lack, to some extent, the evidential character of cases dealt with later, in that the subject of the vision has seldom given a detailed account of the circumstances, but been content, as a rule, to give a general corroboration to the narrative of Miss A.

Among the best reported cases is one in which Sir Joseph Barnby was the chief witness. He had gone to Longford Castle for a wedding, leaving Lady Barnby at Eastbourne. One day, between the

14th and 19th of August 1889, Miss A, says Sir Joseph Barnby, looked in her crystal, and described a bedroom. She appeared to be viewing the room from just outside the open door, for she said :

" If there is a bed in the room it must be behind the door to the left " ; in any case the room was a long one, and the end was occupied by a large window, which formed the entire end of the room. She added : " There is a lady in the room drying her hands on a towel." She described her as tall, dark, slightly foreign in appearance, and with rather " an air " about her. This described with such astonishing accuracy my wife and the room she was then occupying that I was impelled to ask for particulars as to dress, etc. She stated that the dress was of serge, with a good deal of braid on the bodice, and a strip of braid down one side of the skirt. This threw me off the scent, as my wife had expressed regret before I started for Longford that she had not a serge dress with her. My astonishment, therefore, was great on returning to Eastbourne to find my wife wearing a serge dress exactly answering to the description given above. The sequel to this incident comes some sixteen months later on, when my wife and I were attending a performance given by the " Magpie Minstrels " (a society of musical amateurs) at Princes' Hall, Piccadilly. We arrived early, and after placing my wife in a seat I moved about the room speaking to friends here and there. In the course of ten minutes or so Lady Radnor and Miss A. entered the room. During the greetings which ensued Miss A. called my attention to a standing figure, saying : " You will remember my seeing a lady in her bedroom while I was lookng in my crystal ; that is the lady I saw." That was my wife. I need only add that she had never seen my wife.

(Signed)   JOSEPH BARNBY.

Lady Barnby, writing in the same month as her husband, three years after the event, makes the following statement :—

The account about me and my dress is remarkable, as being

out of the general course of things, in this way : I had been re-
marking to Sir Joseph that it was a mistake to come to the
seaside without a serge dress, that being a material particularly
suited for wear at the seaside, but I added : " I do not think
it is much use ordering one now as Madame D. will be gone for
her holiday, it being August." Sir Joseph left the next day
for Longford, and I wrote to Madame D., telling her to make me
the gown. She got the letter on Tuesday (13th Aug. 1889), and
in the marvellously short time by Saturday I received the gown·
Then, again, it is not usual in a hotel to have one's bedroom door
open when one is occupying the room, but the reason for it on this
occasion was the fact that I was to meet Sir Joseph on his return from Longford (Tuesday, 20th Aug. 1889)—as a surprise, in
the new serge gown—and having no clock in our bedroom, which
was at the end of the corridor, with my daughter's room at an
angle to ours, where she slept with her maid, I—thinking I was
somewhat late for meeting the train—opened the door to call
the maid to tell me the time as I washed my hands standing
at the washhand-stand in a line with the open door. I do not
suppose I have ever done such a thing at a hotel before or since.*
(Signed) EDITH MARY BARNBY.

Although this narrative was first written three
years after the event, it is important to notice that
the dates were confirmed by Lady Barnby's diary,
and that the maid confirms the statement as to the
dress being first worn on 20th August.

The superior person will probably dismiss the
whole story as unworthy of credence ; this is the
familiar, short, and easy method with unfortunate
facts. If it were permissible to simplify the universe by excluding from the category of existing
things all that does not tally with our idea of the
universe as it should be, matters would be vastly

* *Proc. S.P.R.* viii. 505 *et seq.*

less complicated than they are. Every German
professor of philosophy—there are forty-eight of
them, each with a system of his own, not to speak
of those who are dead and gone and those who
hope to step into the shoes of the present professors
—would rejoice in the consciousness that his system
was unassailable because the universe was what
he made it (many of them seem to believe this to
be the case now), and there would be at least eight
and forty different universes in Germany alone.
This method, admirable as it is from an abstract
point of view, is not, however, found to give good
results in practice. Consequently it may be questioned whether a simple denial of the truth of this
and all similar stories is an ideal method of dealing
with the facts of experience, whether it be adopted
by the " man of science " or the common or garden
individual who knows all about it.

It may be remarked in passing that when men of
science condescend to offer some remarks on the
subject of psychical research they are frequently
unfortunate, if not downright inaccurate. Professor Ray Lankester recently wrote to *The Times*
to accuse Sir Oliver Lodge of wilfully deceiving the
public by alleging that the S.P.R. had discovered
telepathy, whereas, in fact, no such thing had been
discovered. In such cases the logic is sometimes
on a par with the tone of the assailant, and Professor
Ray Lankester's assault merely served to show

that he did not know the meaning of the word telepathy, which is no more a thing than gravitation is a thing. But this is by the way.

If we do not put Miss A's crystal vision out of the way by declaring that the parties concerned developed concordant hallucinatory memories it hardly appears possible to explain it as the result of coincidence. As Lady Barnby explains, the circumstances were distinctly exceptional ; they might indeed, with the exception of the open door, have been in her mind, and the case thus reduced to one of telepathy *à trois*, if the open door business were an everyday occurrence. But this anticipation of a certain moment is too distinctive a feature of the vision for it to be possible to get rid of the premonitory element in this way. Moreover, the story by no means stands alone. I have recently heard of another case, in which altogether exceptional incidents with regard to the purchase of a house were foretold by a crystal vision three weeks before they became facts. More than one case has been made known at private meetings of the S.P.R., where even more elaborate predictions than that of Miss A's have been made by automatic writing months before they came off, and under circumstances that precluded the possibility of errors as to dates, for these predictions were in the hands of others before the event ; yet they afforded no loophole for the ordinary cause, even if we include among ordinary causes telepathic hypnotism, for statements were made as to a person of whose name the writer was not aware; there could, then, have been no element of mental suggestion in the causation of the acts. Professor Ray Lankester will, doubtless, be prepared to charge all concerned with deliberate fraud, even without waiting to hear the details; but, then, Professor Ray Lankester knows all about the universe, and was quite sure twenty years ago, even before trying any experiments, that there was no such thing as telepathy; or, to be more accurate, no process to which such a designation can properly be applied.

If I had any doubts as to the fact of such premonitions being part of the order of nature my doubts would be removed by an incident in my own experience in which the premonition, which was reported to me on the day on which it was communicated to my informant, related to two incidents in my own life : of these one might have been foreseen by one person, who was not, however, present when the fortune-teller, who had never seen me, gave her " prophecy "; the other, on the other hand, was not predictable by anyone, so far as I can judge, in the ordinary course of things. Both the foretold incidents, I may say, struck me at the time as extremely unlikely.

An interesting account of an experiment, recorded

with unusual though not excessive, still less superfluous, promptitude, was tried in Russia by Miss
Gernet, an associate of the S.P.R. The other persons present were a Miss Klado, a private medium,
who also wrote good books for children (of quality,
however, inferior to her mediumistic performances),
and an English lady, Miss T., from whom the hoped-
for thought transference was to take place.*

The speculum was a glass of water, near which
were two high candles lighted so as to give the necessary brilliant spot to gaze at in the glass (this is
not usually found requisite ; the conditions suggest
that the lady was in the habit of inducing some
degree of autohypnosis ; she believes, however,
that she remains in the normal state). It was
agreed that Miss T. was to think of a lady, name
not mentioned, and, besides, unknown to the percipient, whose surroundings were, the statement
says, " a mystery," or, in plain English, likewise
unknown. Of the lady selected Miss T. herself
knew little, never having been to her house, and
being unacquainted with her mode of life.

After ten or twelve minutes the usual very small
picture formed in the brilliant circle thrown by the
lights on the glass, which stood on a smooth, white
paper. It was characteristic of Miss Gernet's
pictures that they were usually black and white,
with no colour save the natural flesh colouring.

* *Jl. S.P.R.* iii. 71 *et seq.*

First she saw a slender woman with very fair hair, and in a costume which puzzled me as to her doings. I described *à mesure* all that went on in the glass, Miss T. saying nothing as yet. The figure then began to move, and I could then make out that she was dressing ; she walked down the room, lifted her arms, took something from a board, then stayed in front of what was probably a mirror (I saw only the dark side), and dressed her hair on her forehead. Then she washed her hands, and the moving to and fro from me of her arms and of the *essuie-main* she held was perfectly distinct. She had a tea-gown of light colour with long (Greek) sleeves.

The scene changed all at once. I saw her in another room, better lighted, and a gentleman stood beside her, to whom she seemed to talk in an animated way. The gentleman was inclined to be stout, with a light beard and hair a shade darker. When it came to this Miss T. burst out laughing, and said : '' Now I believe in it.''

The description of the lady fitted to an extraordinary degree, and in the gentleman Miss T. recognised one of her relatives, who was reported to be a devoted admirer of the lady.

The narrative goes on to say that at this point the scryer realised that she was intruding on a neighbour's private life, and she broke off the experiment. She adds that Miss T. inquired of another relative of hers if the devoted admirer had paid his respects on the previous evening, and was told that he had done so, and was received by the lady in a light gown with long sleeves.

To this narrative is appended the corroboration of Miss Klado, who states that the facts were verified on the morrow, that Miss Gernet had no knowledge of the long-sleeved lady, and that the vision was described as it progressed.

Miss T. states that the vision described was of " a slight, fair-haired woman dressed in a morning-gown with wide sleeves, and which seemed to be either white or pale blue " ; then my friend told me she saw the door open, and a gentleman enter the room, and on my friend describing his person I recognised it at once.

The very next day I hastened to the lady's house, and questioned her as to where she was the previous evening, and how she was dressed. She told me that, feeling rather unwell, she remained the whole evening at home in her dressing-room (*i.e.* boudoir), and that she wore a pale blue dressing-gown that had wide sleeves ! On examining her dressing-room I was astonished beyond words to find how very accurate the vision was in every detail of it.

It should be mentioned that this account was written nearly a month after those of Miss Gernet and Miss Klado.

On the whole, these narratives are in agreement, in spite of the fact that the subject of the vision remained in the same room. On the difficult question of whether a morning-gown can properly be described as a dressing-gown I offer no opinion, but a lady whom I consulted on the question thinks the two conceptions overlap to some extent. Consequently this detail is not necessarily erroneous in one of the accounts.

For the greater number of evidential cases, however, we are indebted to Mr Andrew Lang, and he, again, to a lady, who goes under the name of Miss Angus.

I refrain from quoting at length all the cases published by Mr Lang in " The Making of Religion," and *The Monthly Review* (Dec. 1901), which form some of the best evidence for telepathy yet published.   Miss Angus writes :

A lady one day asked me to scry out a friend of whom she would think.   Almost immediately I exclaimed : " Here is an old, old lady looking at me with a triumphant smile on her face.   She has a very prominent nose, and nutcracker chin. Her face is very much wrinkled, especially at the sides of her eyes, as if she were always smiling.   She is wearing a little white shawl with a black edge.   But ! she can't be old, as her hair is quite brown ! although her face looks so very, very old." The picture then vanished, and the lady said that I had accurately described her friend's mother instead of himself ; that it was a family joke that the mother must dye her hair, as it was so brown, and she was eighty-two years old.   The lady asked me if the vision were distinct enough for me to recognise the likeness in the son's photograph ; next day she laid several before me, and in a moment, without the slightest hesitation, I picked him out from his wonderful likeness to my vision.*

The inquirer, says Mr Lang, verbally corroborated all the facts to me within a week, and subsequently read and confirmed the account quoted above.

On another occasion Miss Angus says :

One afternoon I was sitting beside a young lady whom I had never before seen or heard of.   She asked if she might look into my crystal, and while she did so I happened to look over her shoulder, and saw a ship tossing on a very heavy, choppy sea, although land was still visible in the dim distance.   That

---

* Lang, *Making of Religion*, p. 69.

vanished, and as suddenly a little house appeared, with five or six (I forget now the exact number I then counted) steps leading up to the door. On the second step stood an old man reading a newspaper. In the front of the house was a field of thick, stubbly grass, where some lambs, I was going to say, but they were more like very small sheep, . . . were grazing. When the scene vanished the young lady told me I had vividly described a spot in Shetland where she and her mother were soon going to spend a few weeks.*

Mr Lang states that this case was communicated to him within a day or two of its occurrence, and again confirmed by the other lady. He was aware, of his own knowledge, that both ladies were perfect strangers.

Another case given by Miss Angus is as follows. It is attested, it may be said, by a friend of the Angus family, the person mainly concerned, who had, however, only seen Miss Angus once before. He was a civilian ; the importance of this will be seen when the story is read.

Miss Angus says :

I had only met Mr —— the day before, and knew almost nothing about him and his personal friends.

I took up the ball, which immediately became misty, and out of this mist a cloud of people appeared, but too indistinctly for me to recognise anything, until suddenly a man on horseback came galloping along. I remember saying : " I can't describe what he is like, but he is dressed in a very queer way, in something so bright that the sun shining on him quite dazzles me, and I cannot make him out ! " As he came nearer I exclaimed :

---

* Lang, *Making of Religion*, p. 97.

" Why, it's a soldier in shining armour ; but it's not an officer, only a soldier ! " Two friends who were in the room (afterwards) said Mr ——'s excitement was intense, and my attention was drawn from the ball by hearing him say : " It's wonderful ! It's perfectly true ! I was thinking of a young boy, the son of a crofter, in whom I am deeply interested, and who is a trooper in the ——, in London, which would account for the crowd of people round him in the street." *

This account was given to Mr Lang some three months after the event. The *prima facie* agent wrote his narrative in December of the same year ; and after mentioning that the subject of crystal gazing had come up apropos of Mr Lang's gift of a crystal a short time previously he goes on : " I fixed my mind upon a friend, a young trooper, as I thought his would be a striking and peculiar personality owing to his uniform, and also because I felt sure Miss Angus could not possibly know of his existence."

Bearing in mind the ease with which the Egyptian magician seems to control the visions of his subjects, we must, of course, treat with great caution any evidence for collective crystal visions, as for visions in general, though to a less extent, unless it is clear that the percipients were on their guard against the possibilities of suggestion ; or unless, which is better still, the experiment were tried under the supervision of a competent experimenter, who recorded all the conversation. †

If the record of the following case is correct, it

* Lang, *Making of Religion*, p. 99. † *Jl.* x. 135.

seems clear that there was no scope for suggestion ; but it must be observed that the three months and a half which elapsed after the vision before it was recorded were quite enough to permit all sorts of hallucinatory memories to grow up, quite unconsciously, round the incident.

Miss G——, a niece of Mr Lang, and Miss C—— were reading anatomy together, and both looked into the crystal together, wondering if they would see the same picture. "At the same moment," goes on Miss G——, " the ball darkened, a white cloud came over the whole, and three pyramids appeared, a large one in front, the other two behind. Then a train of camels, some with riders, others led, passed from left to right, and disappeared behind the large pyramid. The vision lasted about one minute, and vanished simultaneously for both of us. We each wrote down as the things appeared, so as to be quite sure, and I had no thought of pyramids in my mind."

Miss C——'s account agrees as to the picture, but omits the statement as to contemporary notes and as to the simultaneous disappearance of both visions. She goes on to describe an experience which shows that she has the faculty of vivid visualisation and is able to transfer her pictures to the crystal—a dangerous faculty for a co-percipient in a joint crystal vision, if the experience is to count as evidential.

K

It does not appear from Miss G——'s narrative whether the contemporary notes were utilised in preparing the published account. Judging by the common practice in such cases, having satisfied themselves that their records agreed in essentials, it might be imagined that the ladies threw them into the fire, oblivious of the fact that contemporary records are what psychical researchers are always demanding and insisting on. This is, however, not the case. With unusual care they merely mislaid them. Quite apart from this there is some confusion in the statements as to how the record was made. It is the usual experience that a crystal picture vanishes if the eyes are moved from the ball, or even if the eyes are moved in any way, as we have already seen in the case of Miss Angus. How, then, were these ladies able to write down their vision bit by bit as it changed, and all in the space of a minute ? It would have been much more satisfying if we had been told how far the original record was used in the published account and how the original record was made. Of course, it is quite easy to record without removing the eyes from the ball, if you have pencil and paper and can write without looking at the writing. But, then, it should have been stated that these preparations were made, and that the record was made in this way. Against the supposition that the record was made in this way tells the fact that the ladies were looking up muscles, and possibly had no paper at hand ; for, according to Miss C——, the crystal was on the table, and they looked into it casually, and not of set purpose.

These points did not, of course, escape the watchful eye of the editor of *The Journal*, and Miss G—— was duly cross-questioned. A week after the date of the printed account she stated that the rough notes had been left at the college, and could not be found. She now stated that the descriptions were written immediately after seeing the vision, and without previously comparing notes on the subject.

The notes were not, therefore, written bit by bit, as the first account suggested. This small but important variation cannot but raise some doubt as to the accuracy of the recollections in general. A question which does not seem to have suggested itself to the editor of *The Journal* was whether the percipients had seen any picture of a pyramid which might have suggested the same idea to each without a pyramid being actually in the mind of either. As a matter of fact they had not, but the ladies were occupied with muscles, and may well have turned their attention, amongst others, to the atrophied and inconstant *pyramidalis abdominis*. This would have been quite sufficient to suggest a pyramid. Mr Myers records a case where a man going along the streets of Paris saw on a door, as he

imagined, Verbascum Thapsus. Much puzzled by
the appearance of these words in such a place he
retraced his steps, to find that he had actually seen
the word bouillon ; the scientific name of the plant
bouillon blanc is the Latin name quoted above. If
the subliminal is agile enough to jump from bouillon
to Verbascum Thapsus it is no very long leap from
pyramidalis to pyramid.

We have seen above that a mirror is frequently
employed instead of a crystal ; in particular,
Catherine de Medici is said to have been shown all
the kings of France in a mirror at Chaumont.
Apropos of this story, it was pointed out that there
was little or no evidence for it, and that the most
natural explanation was trickery. Since the passage was written a case of extraordinary interest
has been published in the *Journal of the S.P.R.*,
which we quote in full below. It will be seen
that it bears a very close resemblance to the
supposed vision of Catherine de Medici. At the
same time, the mere fact that an analogous case
can be quoted does not do much to diminish
the probability of trickery in the castle of Chaumont.

The recent case referred to was sent to the *S.P.R.*
by an Associate of the Society, Mrs H. J. Wilson, who
is intimately acquainted with all the witnesses,
whose full names have been given to the officials

of the Society. Mrs C——, the medium mentioned, is not a professional medium, but a friend of the other ladies.

The incident took place in May 1904, and the first account is from a letter written shortly afterwards by Mrs A—— to Mrs Wilson, as follows :—

It was in my bedroom at B——, Switzerland. Mrs C—— was the medium. She was seated facing the long mirror in my wardrobe, and we—that is, C—— [Mrs P——, sister of Mrs A——], A—— [the daughter of Mrs A——], Mrs H——, and myself—were seated just behind her, also facing the mirror. Mrs C—— was not in trance. In a very short time we saw my father's face form over Mrs C——'s face (in the mirror), and then S——'s face, two or three times following. She was smiling, and looking hard at us, her two sisters. Then she faded away, and a long corridor came, with a large hall or room at the end of it, brilliantly lighted up. Many figures were walking about, but my figure and E——'s [Mrs A——'s son] were the most prominent—there was no mistaking them. I recognised my own figure walking about, and leaning forward to talk. That was all, as it was rather late, and time to go to bed.

S——, the sister of Mrs A—— and Mrs P——, had died in March, 1904 ; E——, the son of Mrs A——, was living at the time, and in London.

The account of the other sister, Mrs P——,was dictated by her to Mrs Wilson, and sent enclosed in a letter from Mrs Wilson, dated 3rd October 1904. It is as follows :—

It was at B——, about 1st May 1904, at 8.30 P.M. The electric light was full on all the time, shaded only by a piece of silver tissue paper. There were present Mrs C——(the medium), Mrs A——, A——, Mrs H——, and myself. Mrs C—— sat in front

of a mirror, Mrs A—— and I sat just behind her, and the other
two to right and left of us respectively. Behind us was the
bedroom wall, and a washing-stand against that, with a small
mirror over it. The medium was not entranced. I saw S——'s
face form on Mrs C——'s face, followed by that of old Mrs P——.
Then came a full-length figure of my father in the mirror, in his
robes, very like the portrait. He looked benignant and *rested*,
with lines of face much smoothed away. This faded, and then
all perceived a long passage in the mirror, at a guess about twenty-
five feet long, with bay window at the end, and sunshine
streaming through. There was a window-seat, and two figures
standing by it, unrecognisable. Then a third figure appeared, also
unrecognisable. They seemed to look out of window, and
converse. Medium then became tired.

The next account, written in October 1904, is
from Miss A——, and is as follows :—

Mother, Mrs C——, Aunt C——[Mrs P——], another lady, and
myself, were all seated in front of a large pier-glass, Mrs C——
(the medium) being slightly nearer the glass (say three inches)
than the rest of us. The gas was turned down to about half its
strength. Presently, after sitting ten minutes or so, we saw
what appeared to be a white mist rising up in front of the
medium's reflection, and it finally resolved into a good and
distinct likeness of granddad. When we recognised it the figure
smiled and nodded its head. Then a likeness of Aunt S—— appeared, not so distinct, but perfectly easy of recognition ; after
which a lady appeared unknown to four of us, but recognised by
the lady who was sitting with us.

For a time we saw nothing but mist again ; but it gradually
cleared, and a long corridor became visible, with a door at the
farther end evidently opened inward, and screened on the side
nearest us by looped curtains, through which we saw into a
brilliantly-lighted room, whether bright sunlight or artificial light
we could not tell. Figures too distant to be recognised came
and went in the room, and once a girl in what appeared to be
bridal dress stood just behind the opening of the curtain. Then

the doors appeared to be shut for a time, but presently opened, and two figures pushed aside the curtains, and came down the corridor towards us, talking. We recognised them as mother and E——. Then the picture faded again, and we closed the sitting. This is to the best of my recollection, but as I took no notes at the time I may easily have forgotten details.

In answer to further questions Miss A—— wrote :

14th October 1904.

The likenesses were formed on Mrs C——'s image in the glass, as it were, transforming her features into those of the persons represented. Her own face, as distinct from the image, was unchanged, except that the eyes were closed, while the faces in the glass all had their eyes open. This is an interesting point, I think.

The fourth witness, Mrs H——, dictated her account to Mrs Wilson in the early part of November 1904, as follows :—

I first saw the head and shoulders of an old clergyman with grey hair—no beard ; he wore the old-fashioned " Geneva bands " that the clergy used to wear. I did not recognise him, but heard Mrs P—— and Mrs A—— say it was their father. I did not see him on the medium's face, but in a corner of the mirror apart from the medium. I also heard Mrs P—— and Mrs A—— say that they saw their sister, but I did not see her. After this we saw a ballroom in the mirror, very brightly lighted, with people walking about in it. I did not recognise any of them. I ought to have said that at first I saw a curtain across the room, and it was when it was withdrawn that I saw the people walking about.

The room we were sitting in was lighted by a candle.

The Editor of the *Journal* says : " It is unfortunate that the witnesses did not record their impressions at the time, or immediately afterwards,

since it is clear that in some respects their present
recollections are not quite correct. Thus Mrs P——
says : ' The electric light was full on all the time,
shaded only by a piece of silver tissue paper.' Miss
A—— says : ' The gas was turned down to about
half its strength.' Mrs H—— says : ' The room we
were sitting in was lighted by a candle.' One or
other of these descriptions must be inaccurate, unless all of them are incomplete. It must, however,
be remembered that we hardly ever find two people
giving exactly the same description even of ordinary
events, and we very seldom have the opportunity
of comparing together as many as four independent
accounts of the same occurrence. Whenever we
did this we should probably find quite as much
disagreement as in the present case.

" When we come to the descriptions of the figures
seen in the mirror the discrepancies are far more
marked. There is, of course, no proof of inaccuracy
in this, because it is quite possible—not to say
probable—that the hallucinations were not the same
to all the percipients. Miss A—— is the only one
who describes the appearance of a white mist in the
mirror preceding the appearance of the figures.
(Our readers will remember that this appearance is
a familiar experience with crystal gazers whether
as a preliminary to subjective or to veridical visions.)
With regard to the individual figures seen—(1) As
to the father of Mrs A—— and Mrs P——, Mrs

A—— and Miss A—— say that they saw his face form over Mrs C——'s face in the mirror, Miss A—— adding that the figure smiled, and nodded its head. Mrs P—— describes a full-length figure of her father in the mirror, in his robes, the figure having no connection with the medium's reflection in the mirror. Mrs H—— describes the head and shoulders of an old clergyman with grey hair and ' Geneva bands,' ' not on the medium's face, but in a corner of the mirror, apart from the medium.' (2) The sister of Mrs A—— and Mrs P—— was seen by both of them and by Miss A—— in a similar manner—her face forming over the medium's face in the mirror—but not seen at all by Mrs H——, though she heard the others saying they had seen it. (3) ' Old Mrs P——' is mentioned only by Mrs P——. (4) An unrecognised lady is described only by Miss A——. (5) In the scene of the long corridor, with a brilliantly-lighted room at the end, and figures walking about in it, all the figures were unrecognised, except those of Mrs A—— and her son, which were recognised and described (though somewhat differently) by Mrs A—— herself and her daughter.

" These various discrepancies may arise either from actual dissimilarities in the hallucinations, perhaps from inaccuracies in the recollections of the witnesses, or possibly from a combination of both causes ; but, however this may be, there seems no doubt that the hallucinations were to a great extent similar. The case then affords a striking proof of the possibility—so often denied—of producing hallucinations in several persons at once by mere suggestion and expectancy, without hypnosis or any such process. No verbal suggestion even was employed by the medium ; for Mrs Wilson, having made special inquiries on this point, tells us that Mrs C—— closed her eyes, and did not speak during the sitting ; the sitters, however, did describe what they were seeing to one another during the time of the vision.

" The case may also tend to throw light on what is stated to occur with more than one professional medium—when the so-called ' materialised form ' is recognised by one sitter as the medium masquerading, while another recognises it at the same time as the figure of a deceased friend." *

So far the Editor of the *Journal*. There are various other points which seem to call for remark. It is not quite clear from the narrative of Mrs P—— whether as the commentary in the *Journal* supposes, the figure of her father was independent of the medium ; it seems not impossible that it may have completely occulted the medium's reflection ; at any rate nothing is said of the medium having been visible simultaneously. It would be interesting to know whether the corner in which Mrs H—— saw this same figure was the corner in which she, sitting not ex-

* *Jl.* xii., 17 *et seq.*

actly in front, would have seen an external object reflected when Mrs P—— saw the same object reflected in (?) the centre of the mirror. There is, of course, no reason to suppose that there was any external object, nor even any hallucination independent of the mirror ; moreover, even if there were any hallucinatory form in such a position that a reflection would be produced, if it were a real object, it by no means follows that a reflection will be seen. It is, nevertheless, of some interest to know how the figure in question behaved.

It is, of course, possible that the asymmetrical position of the figure is simply a later addition, due to the fact that the percipients compared notes, and that Mrs H—— assumed that the mirror figure must have behaved as a real reflection would have done under the circumstances. But there is nothing to show that any such idea crossed her mind, and it does not appear to have suggested itself to any of the other percipients. On the other hand we might, if we had contemporary notes, find that similar variations of position were present in all or many of the other cases. In the absence, however, of details as to the size of the mirror, the distance of the percipients from it, and their distance from each other, it is difficult to discuss these questions, even from the hypothetical point of view rendered necessary by the absence of contemporary notes.

The importance of this case is manifest. Even

making the utmost allowance for hallucinatory memory, it is impossible to deny that several persons simultaneously saw persons and scenes in the mirror; and it is straining the hypothesis of hallucinatory memory very far to deny that these persons and scenes were anything but largely identical in the case of at least three of the percipients; for, be it remarked, if hallucinatory memory suggested to the three percipients that they had seen their relatives in the mirror, it should equally have suggested to the fourth that she saw *her* relatives; excitement and all the other familiar theories will not explain why one of the ladies present saw only unrecognised figures.

However, even granting that hallucinatory memory will explain how Mrs A——, Mrs P——, and Miss A—— all state that they saw their relatives in the mirror, there is still evidence for telepathy. It is expressly stated that there was no verbal suggestion except from the percipients, and yet all the persons present who looked at the mirror saw something. At a high estimate, the number of crystal gazers is something like five per cent.; the chances are, therefore, very considerable against four persons of a party possessing the faculty, even though three of them belong to the same family.

For those, however, for whom the hypothesis of hallucinatory memory is an unsatisfactory explanation, and who regard a telepathic explanation as more probable, the case is of the highest importance. Not only does it afford a satisfactory explanation, as is pointed out in the remarks quoted from the *Journal*, of discrepancies in the reports of seances, but it affords decisive proof that collectivity is a character which may be associated with visions due to human agency only, and consequently disposes of collectivity as a test of " real " ghosts. These and other conclusions, however, do not concern us here.

On the whole, fragmentary as it is, and unsatisfactory in that we have no records from unsuccessful scryers or of their proportion to successful scryers, the evidence for telepathic crystal visions seems strong. The arguments against thought transference have been discussed elsewhere,* and it is useless to recapitulate here what has been said at length in another work. I propose to sum up the evidence for telepathy after dealing with ghosts, deathwraiths, and other spontaneous phenomena of a *prima-facie* telepathic character.

* See *Thought Transference,* by the same author.

CHAPTER XII

BUT few directions are necessary for the experimenter. The necessity of an exact contemporaneous record has been insisted upon sufficiently frequently in the course of the present work. Best of all is for some one to take down the scryer's description *à mésure*; next best for the scryer to dictate or write it immediately after the scry; but this is useless where collective gazing is being attempted. The verification of the visions is a matter of some difficulty. If the scryer has no difficulty in seeing his or her friends let a time be fixed and a diary kept by the persons to be seen in the vision, with a careful record of hours and minutes, goings and comings, dress, and the like.

As we have seen, however, the crystal is apt to anticipate events, and then we can only trust to luck. Sometimes it looks some time into the past, and then we can only trust to diaries and recollections. It is, however, worth while to try for a good contemporary vision, and to make arrangements that will leave no loophole if it comes off.

I shall be pleased to receive from any scryers who

will favour me with their results, reports and corroborations, authenticated by names, dates, and places, not necessarily for publication, but as a warrant of good faith.

It is well to get any who are present during the scry to corroborate the circumstances as far as in them lies. It must not be forgotten that suggestion is a very powerful factor, and any person present who recognises the scene or persons of the vision should give no hint of it, much less ask leading questions. It sometimes happens that the scryer is too absorbed in the vision, and needs prompting. This should be done by someone who has neither part nor lot in the scenes represented.

Crystals can be obtained of the Society for Psychical Research, 20 Hanover Square, London, W., to whose care reports of crystal gazing may be consigned to me.

I have sometimes heard it suggested that crystal gazing is injurious. I can only say that some of the most normal persons I know are excellent crystal gazers, and moderate indulgence in the sport is no more harmful than an after-dinner snooze.

BIBLIOGRAPHY

The most important modern works and articles dealing with crystal gazing are :

ANDREW LANG, " Making of Religion."
ANDREW LANG in *Monthly Review*, 1901.
MISS X——, " Essays in Psychical Research."
Proc. S.P.R. viii., 458-535.
Proc. S.P.R. viii., 259-276.
Proc. S.P.R. v., 486-521.

For some telepathic experiments see the volume in this series on experimental thought transference.

INDEX

L   161